Babe: Here's so ———
spicy, just like
Enjoy 'creating' the:

Your Ever Hu . o   x-mas.
Andy Food !! ___ '97

C000302441

HOT & SPICY COOKBOOK

CHARMAINE SOLOMON

Photography
Ray Joyce

Illustrations
Barbara Rodanska

LEOPARD

This edition published in 1995 by Leopard Books,
a division of Random House UK Ltd,
20 Vauxhall Bridge Road, London SW1V 2SA

First published in 1990 by Murdoch Books,
a division of Murdoch Magazines Pty Ltd,
213 Miller Street, North Sydney NSW 2060

Printed by New Interlitho, Italy
Typeset by Savage Type Pty Ltd, Brisbane, Qld

ISBN 0 7529 0155 9

The publisher wishes to thank the following:

Exotic Fruit Groves, Queensland
Limoges Australia
Noritake Australia
Villeroy & Boch Australia
Wardlaw Pty Ltd
Waterford Wedgwood Australia

A NOTE TO COOKS

The recipes in this book use a combination of metric weights
and, for some dry and liquid ingredients, cup measures.
Cooks wishing to use Imperial weights, or who are
unfamiliar with cup measures, should consult the
Conversion Chart before attempting any of the recipes.

COOKERY RATING

easy

a little care needed

for confident cooks

CONTENTS

CONVERSION CHART

WEIGHTS AND MEASURES

Australian and American cooks use standard measuring cups for liquids and many solids, including flour, sugar, cocoa powder and prepared vegetables and fruits, whereas British cooks favour measuring jugs calibrated in millilitres and fluid ounces and scales calibrated in both metric and Imperial measures. The chart that follows gives equivalent metric, Imperial and standard cup measures. Please note that an American pint is equivalent to 16 fl oz whereas a British pint is 20 fl oz.

LIQUID MEASURES

Metric	Imperial	Standard Cup Measure
30 mL	1 fl oz	
60 mL	2 fl oz	¼ cup
75 mL	2½ fl oz	
80 mL	2¾ fl oz	⅓ cup
90 mL	3 fl oz	
125 mL	4 fl oz	½ cup
155 mL	5 fl oz	
170 mL	5½ fl oz	⅔ cup
185 mL	6 fl oz	¾ cup
220 mL	7 fl oz	
250 mL	8 fl oz	1 cup (½ US pint)
280 mL	9 fl oz	
315 mL	10 fl oz (½ pint)	1¼ cups
350 mL	11 fl oz	1⅓ cups
375 mL	12 fl oz	1½ cups
410 mL	13 fl oz	1⅔ cups
440 mL	14 fl oz	1¾ cups
470 mL	15 fl oz	
500 mL	16 fl oz	2 cups (1 US pint)
600 mL	20 fl oz (1 pint)	2½ cups
750 mL	1 pint 5 fl oz	3 cups
1 litre	1 pint 12 fl oz	4 cups
1.5 litres	2 pints 8 fl oz	6 cups

DRY MEASURES

Metric	Imperial
15 g	½ oz
30 g	1 oz
45 g	1½ oz
60 g	2 oz
90 g	3 oz
125 g	4 oz
155 g	5 oz
185 g	6 oz
220 g	7 oz
250 g	8 oz
280 g	9 oz
315 g	10 oz
350 g	11 oz
375 g	12 oz
410 g	13 oz
440 g	14 oz
470 g	15 oz
500 g	16 oz (1 lb)
750 g	1 lb 8 oz (1½ lb)
1 kg	2¼ lb
1.5 kg	3¼ lb
2 kg	4½ lb
2.5 kg	5½ lb

STANDARD CUP MEASURES

It is not possible to give a single standard cup measure for all dry ingredients as they all weigh different amounts; a cup of breadcrumbs, for instance, weighs 60 g/2 oz, whereas a cup of sugar weighs 250 g/8 oz. Some of the more common ingredients traditionally measured by cup in America and/or Australia are listed below:

Cup Measures	Metric/Imperial
1 cup butter or margarine (2 US sticks)	250 g/8 oz
1 cup grated hard cheese	125 g/4 oz
1 cup cream cheese/full fat soft cheese	250 g/8 oz
1 cup crumbled blue vein cheese	125–155 g/4–5 oz
1 cup plain/all-purpose flour	125 g/4 oz
1 cup wholemeal/wholewheat flour	140 g/4½ oz
1 cup crystalline/granulated sugar	250 g/8 oz
1 cup caster/superfine sugar	250 g/8 oz
1 cup icing/confectioners' sugar	155 g/5 oz
1 cup packed brown sugar	185 g/6 oz
1 cup chopped nuts	125 g/4 oz
1 cup soft/fresh breadcrumbs	60 g/2 oz
1 cup dry breadcrumbs	125 g/4 oz
1 cup raw rice	220 g/7 oz
1 cup cooked rice	125 g/4 oz
1 cup desiccated coconut	90 g/3 oz
1 cup cornflakes	25 g/1 oz
1 cup dried fruit (types vary)	155–185 g/5–6 oz
1 cup cooked mashed pumpkin	350 g/11 oz
1 cup pasta shapes	125 g/4 oz
1 cup chopped tomatoes	185 g/6 oz
1 cup chopped onion	125 g/4 oz
1 cup chopped capsicum/sweet pepper	125 g/4 oz
1 cup sliced mushrooms	125 g/4 oz
1 cup shelled peas	170 g/5½ oz
1 cup diced raw potato	185 g/6 oz
1 cup mashed potato	250 g/8 oz
1 cup diced apple	125 g/4 oz
1 cup apple purée (applesauce)	250 g/8 oz
1 cup black or redcurrants or blueberries	125 g/4 oz
1 cup raspberries or small strawberries	155 g/5 oz
1 cup honey, syrup or jam	350–375 g/11–12 oz
1 cup minced/ground beef or pork	250 g/8 oz

STANDARD SPOON MEASURES

When measuring by teaspoon (tsp) or tablespoon (tbsp), always use standard metric measuring spoons. While these are the same for Britain and the US (5 mL and 15 mL respectively), please note that the Australian standard tablespoon holds 20 mL and is therefore equivalent to 4 standard teaspoons. As recipes for this book were tested in Australia, British and American readers will need to adjust tablespoon quantities.

Australia	UK	US
1 tsp (5 mL)	1 tsp (5 mL)	1 tsp (5 mL)
1 tbsp (20 mL)	1 tbsp (15 mL)	1 tbsp (15 mL)

LINEAR MEASURES

5 mm	¼ in
1 cm	½ in
2 cm	¾ in
2.5 cm	1 in
5 cm	2 in
6 cm	2½ in
8 cm	3 in
10 cm	4 in
12 cm	5 in
15 cm	6 in
18 cm	7 in
20 cm	8 in
23 cm	9 in
25 cm	10 in
28 cm	11 in
30 cm	12 in
46 cm	18 in
50 cm	20 in
61 cm	24 in
77 cm	30 in

OVEN TEMPERATURES

	°C	°F	Gas Mark
Very slow	120	250	½
Slow	150	300	1–2
Mod. slow	160	325	3
Moderate	180	350	4
Mod. hot	190	375	5–6
Hot	200	400	6–7
Very hot	230	450	8–9

Dips, Nibbles, Savouries & Snacks

This chapter contains a wide-ranging assortment of recipes with just one thing in common — they are savoury and spicy. As for when you serve them, that's up to you . . . with pre-dinner drinks, when someone drops in and you want just a light, tasty offering, or when you suddenly find yourself starving and dinner's not for another hour or two. Some are for immediate consumption, others can be stored in an airtight container, while the dips do well in the refrigerator. Still others may be frozen (curry puffs, meatballs) and cooked or heated just before serving, a truly versatile selection.

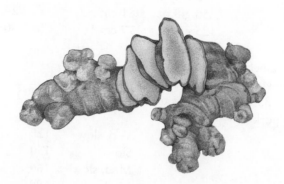

Clockwise from back: Cheese Sambousek (page 21), Chilli Prawns (page 10), Guacamole and Nachos (page 13)

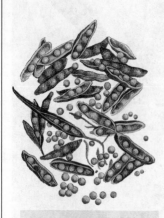

Savoury Cereal and Nut Mix

This cereal mixture is not for breakfast! It's crunchy and spicy hot with Indian flavours — a winner served as a nibble with drinks.

PREPARATION TIME: *10 minutes*
COOKING TIME: *3 minutes*
MAKES *about 5 cups*

2 tablespoons oil
3 dried red chillies, broken into pieces and seeds removed
1 teaspoon black mustard seeds
1 teaspoon garam masala
1 teaspoon salt
½ teaspoon chilli powder
2 teaspoons ground cumin
4 cups crisp, unsweetened cereal such as flaked rice, oat or corn flakes, rice krispies
1 cup roasted peanuts and/or cashews
1 cup potato straws (optional)

1 Heat the oil in a large, deep frying pan or, better still, a wok, and fry the chillies and mustard seeds until the seeds start to pop. Remove from heat, add the garam masala, salt, chilli powder and cumin and mix well.
2 Add the cereal and toss well to distribute salt and spices. Taste for seasoning and add extra salt or chilli if necessary.
3 Stir in the peanuts and potato straws. Cool and store in an airtight container for up to two weeks.

Eggplant Dip

At a high class Lebanese restaurant I tasted this popular dip with a delicious extra flavour — a hint of cumin.

PREPARATION TIME: *45 minutes*
COOKING TIME: *about 30 minutes*
SERVES *4–6*

2 × 500 g firm eggplants
3 cloves garlic, finely chopped
1 teaspoon salt
1 teaspoon ground cumin
¼ cup tahina (sesame seed paste)
½ cup lemon juice
water
chopped parsley

1 Grill the eggplants until the skin is burnt and blackened all over and the eggplants are cooked and so soft that they yield to gentle pressure. This takes about 30 minutes. If you have a gas cooker this can be done directly over the gas flame.
2 Cool and then carefully peel away every bit of skin.
3 Chop and mash the flesh, or purée in a food processor until smooth and add the garlic crushed with salt, the cumin, tahina and lemon juice. Add just enough water to make a dip the consistency of mayonnaise.
4 Spread on a serving plate, sprinkle with parsley and serve with flat Lebanese bread.

Chilli Prawns

Serve small devilled prawns on croûtons as a delicious appetiser.

PREPARATION TIME: *30 minutes*
COOKING TIME: *30 minutes*
SERVES *4–6*

500 g small to medium raw prawns
1½ tablespoons oil
1 large onion, finely chopped
1 clove garlic, finely chopped
1 teaspoon salt
¼ teaspoon chilli powder or to taste
1 teaspoon paprika
¼ teaspoon ground turmeric
1 teaspoon sugar
2 teaspoons tomato paste or sauce

1 Shell and de-vein the prawns.
2 Heat oil in a heavy frying pan and cook onions and garlic over low heat until soft and golden brown, about 15 minutes. As the oil begins to appear around the edges, stir in chilli powder, salt, paprika and turmeric and fry for 1 minute.
3 Add prawns and stir-fry for 3 minutes. Add ¼ cup water, cover pan and simmer on low heat for 5 minutes. Stir in sugar and tomato paste and cook uncovered for a few minutes longer until gravy is dark reddish brown, thick, and dry enough to coat the prawns. Serve on crackers or small squares of fried bread.

When a recipe gives an approximate amount of a spice, use the smaller quantity first and allow time for the flavour to develop. After tasting the dish you may, if you wish, add more, but the role of spices is to enhance the flavour of food, not to disguise or overpower it.

Blachan/trasi/kapi Small blocks of dried shrimp or prawn paste, made from the salted or fermented shellfish.
Galangal Rhizome resembling ginger but with a distinct, slightly peppery flavour. See also Laos.
Kalonji A flavoursome spice, also known as nigella or, colloquially, as onion seeds.
Laos Powdered form of galangal. Not unlike ground ginger in appearance and flavour. 1 teaspoon is equivalent to about 1 cm/½ inch of fresh galangal.
Sambal oelek A fiery Indonesian chilli sauce.
Wasabi Japanese green horseradish mustard. Wasabi is extremely hot.

Coconut Meat Balls

Traditionally in Indonesia these balls are made very small to accompany a meal of rice and curry. I love them for picnics. They may also be made bigger and flatter, like hamburgers, and they can be shallow fried. When making tiny balls it is probably easier to deep fry them.

PREPARATION TIME: *25 minutes*
COOKING TIME: *about 30 minutes*
(4–5 minutes a batch)
MAKES 60 *small balls or 8 large patties*

250 g desiccated coconut
6 or 7 tablespoons hot water
500 g finely minced beef
½ teaspoon dried shrimp paste (trasi or blachan)
2 cloves garlic
½ teaspoon salt
½ teaspoon ground black pepper
1½ teaspoons ground coriander
1 teaspoon ground cumin
½ teaspoon powdered galangal
2 eggs, beaten
peanut oil

1 Put coconut into a bowl and sprinkle with hot water. Stir well with a fork to moisten coconut evenly. Add minced beef.
2 Dissolve the shrimp paste in a tablespoon of hot water. Crush garlic with salt to form a smooth paste.
3 Add all the spices, the garlic and the shrimp paste to the beaten eggs and mix well.
4 Pour egg mixture over meat and coconut in the bowl. Mix and knead well with the hands so that the spices are evenly distributed and mixture becomes smooth.
5 Shape into 60 small balls. Shallow fry, shaking the pan frequently to prevent sticking, or deep fry until crisp and golden brown all over. Drain on absorbent paper.
6 Serve as a cocktail savoury, use to fill crusty bread rolls on a picnic, or include as an accompaniment with a meal of rice and curry.

Savoury Cereal and Nut Mix and Coconut Meat Balls

*Eggplant Dip (page 10)
and Crunchy Wafers*

Crunchy Wafers

Flat breads, readily available at supermarkets, make a quick savoury.

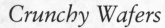

PREPARATION TIME: *20 minutes*
COOKING TIME: *6–8 minutes*
MAKES *24 triangles*

*Lavosh or pita breads (white or
wholemeal)*
2 teaspoons ground cumin
1 teaspoon ground oregano
½ teaspoon chilli powder, optional
1 teaspoon caraway seeds
1 tablespoon sesame seeds
1 teaspoon salt
*1 teaspoon crushed garlic
olive oil*

1 If using pita, separate into two thin layers by cutting around the edge with scissors and gently pulling them apart.
2 Combine the spices and seeds, the crushed garlic and salt. Add enough olive oil to mix to a paste.
3 With a small spatula, spread this mixture thinly on the bread. Cut into triangles.
4 Arrange in a single layer on a baking sheet and bake in a moderate over for 6–8 minutes or until lightly browned and crisp. Remove and cool on a wire rack. Store in an airtight container.

Devilled Nuts

Hot and moreish! You can use a mixture of nuts — cashews, almonds, peanuts — or just a single favourite variety. For more complex flavours, I sometimes use a tablespoon of Creole Seasoning (page 88) instead of the salt and chilli powder.

PREPARATION TIME: *5 minutes*
COOKING TIME: *about 20 minutes (4–5 minutes a batch)*
MAKES *about 4 cups*

500 g raw nuts
oil for deep frying
2 teaspoons salt
2 teaspoons chilli powder

1 Heat oil in a deep frying pan or wok and fry the nuts, a handful at a time, on medium heat, stirring constantly so they colour evenly. When golden, remove with a slotted spoon and drain on absorbent paper.
2 When all the nuts have been fried and drained, combine salt and chilli powder and sprinkle over, tossing well to distribute the flavours. Or if you prefer, use the Creole Seasoning.
3 When cold, dust off excess salt and chilli powder and serve. The nuts will keep for up to a week if stored in an airtight container.

Guacamole

This popular Mexican dip is a mixture of smoothly mashed, bland avocado made exciting with chilli, cumin and other flavours. To keep a good green colour, make guacamole not more than a couple of hours before serving.

PREPARATION TIME: *10 minutes*
COOKING TIME: *nil*
SERVES *6–8*

2 large ripe avocados
1 firm ripe tomato
2 or 3 canned jalapeno chillies or mild green chillies, drained
½ teaspoon ground cumin, optional
1 small onion, finely chopped
2 tablespoons lemon juice

1 tablespoon chopped fresh coriander
1 teaspoon salt
¼ teaspoon pepper

1 Halve the avocados, scoop out flesh from the shells and mash with a stainless fork. Peel, seed and chop the tomato, chop chillies, and mix all the ingredients together.
2 Put the guacamole into a bowl and replace one of the avocado seeds in the dip (it is said to keep it from discolouring). Cover closely with plastic film, pressing it lightly onto the surface. Chill until serving time, then remove seed and serve with corn chips, crackers or crisp vegetables for dipping.

Nachos

To start a meal, or just as a snack. Nachos (pronounced nah-chose with the accent on the first syllable) are quickly put together. The simplest version features corn chips covered with melted cheese. There are more substantial versions with guacamole dip or bean purée between layers of corn chips, also finished with a layer of melted cheese.

PREPARATION TIME: *20 minutes (including time for making Bean Dip)*
COOKING TIME: *5 minutes*
SERVES *6*

1 packet corn chips
1 quantity Pinto Bean Dip (see page 18)
2 cups grated Cheddar cheese
paprika for sprinkling

1 Arrange the corn chips on a heatproof plate, spooning some bean dip and sprinkling cheese between layers. Finish with corn chips and a thick layer of grated cheese.
2 Place under a preheated griller until the cheese melts, bubbles and turns golden. Sprinkle with paprika and serve immediately. Each person pulls individual chips from the pile. This snack is eaten with the fingers.

Devilled Nuts

Honey Spiced Chicken Wings

Suitable to serve as finger food, at a picnic, with drinks or with vegetables as part of a main dish. Serve hot or cold.

PREPARATION TIME: *10 minutes*
plus 1 hour marinating
COOKING TIME: *45 minutes*
SERVES *6–8*

1.5 kg chicken wings
⅓ cup soy sauce
¼ cup peanut oil
1 tablespoon dry sherry
1 teaspoon crushed garlic
¼ teaspoon salt
½ teaspoon finely grated fresh ginger
½ teaspoon five-spice powder
½ cup honey

1 Wash chicken wings and dry well.
2 Discard tips, trim excess skin and divide at joint if liked. In a large shallow dish mix together all remaining ingredients. Place chicken wings in the marinade and turn to coat all sides. Cover and leave to marinate for an hour or more.
3 Preheat oven to moderate (180°C). Remove chicken from marinade, put in a roasting pan in one layer and spoon about 2 tablespoons of the marinade over. Roast in a moderate oven about 45 minutes or until chicken is brown and crisp, basting every 20 minutes with the marinade in the roasting pan.

> Store your spices in airtight glass jars, out of sunlight and heat. I store precious spices such as saffron and cardamom in the freezer and they are wonderfully fragrant even after many years.

Cajun Popcorn

The size of the crisp-fried prawn pieces may remind one of popcorn, but there the resemblance ends. Best served soon after cooking.

PREPARATION TIME: *30 minutes*
COOKING TIME: *10 minutes*
SERVES *4–6*

250 g large raw prawns
1 teaspoon onion powder
1 teaspoon garlic salt
½ teaspoon cayenne or chilli powder
½ teaspoon ground white pepper

¼ teaspoon ground black pepper
¼ teaspoon ground thyme
¼ teaspoon ground oregano
plain flour
1 egg, beaten
dry breadcrumbs
oil for frying

1 Shell and devein the prawns and cut each into 1 cm pieces.
2 Combine the onion powder, garlic salt, ground spices and herbs and mix well with the prawns. Leave for 10 minutes before tossing to coat lightly with flour. Dust off excess flour, then coat with beaten egg and finally roll in breadcrumbs, trying to coat each small piece of prawn separately.
3 Heat oil for deep frying and fry a handful of prawn pieces at a time on medium high heat for 2 minutes or until they are crisp and golden brown. Lift out on a slotted spoon and drain on absorbent paper. Continue frying the remaining pieces and serve as soon as they are done.

Chilli-Cheese Toast

When the refrigerator yields bits and pieces of cheese, grate them all finely and make a spread for thin slices of bread. Crisp in a slow oven and serve warm or cool. Store in an airtight container.

PREPARATION TIME: *15 minutes*
COOKING TIME: *20 minutes*
MAKES *about 18 slices*

day-old French bread or bread rolls
1 cup finely grated tasty cheese
2 tablespoons soft butter
2 teaspoons sweet chilli sauce
½ teaspoon salt
¼ teaspoon cayenne pepper or *hot chilli powder*

1 Cut thin slices from day-old bread and place on a baking tray.
2 Combine the cheese with the rest of the ingredients and mix well. Spread thinly but evenly over the slices of bread, then bake in a slow oven (150°C), for 15–20 minutes or until bread is crisp and dry. Serve at once, or cool thoroughly and store in an airtight container for a few days.

Honey Spiced Chicken Wings, Cajun Popcorn and Chilli-Cheese Toast

Curry Puffs with Mint Chutney (page 87)

Spiced Pecans

Spiced Pecans

These are so quick and easy to make, yet keep everyone reaching for more. Instead of deep frying, the nuts are toasted in the oven and tossed in very little oil which helps the spice mixture to cling.

PREPARATION TIME: *5 minutes*
COOKING TIME: *8–10 minutes*
SERVES 6–8

250 g pecan halves
2 tablespoons chicken stock powder
1 teaspoon chilli powder
1 teaspoon garam masala
½ teaspoon ground black pepper
½ teaspoon ground turmeric
1 teaspoon garlic salt
2 tablespoons salad oil

1 Spread the pecan halves on a baking tray and bake in a moderate oven (180°C), for about 8 minutes or until lightly toasted.
2 Meanwhile, combine the chicken stock powder, spices and garlic salt.
3 Heat the oil in a wok or large frying pan and toss the toasted pecans in it until lightly coated. Remove from the heat, sprinkle combined ingredients over and toss until all the nuts have some of the spicy and salty flavours clinging to them. Cool completely before storing in an airtight container for up to one week.

Curry Puffs

These small deep-fried pastries are a favourite in North India, where curries are known for their fragrant spiciness rather than pungency and heat.

PREPARATION TIME: *30 to 45 minutes*
COOKING TIME: *1 hour plus 15 minutes for deep-frying (1–2 minutes a batch of 6)*
MAKES *about 36*

1 tablespoon oil or ghee
2 medium onions, finely chopped
1 fresh red or green chilli, seeded and chopped
½ teaspoon crushed garlic
2 teaspoons finely chopped fresh ginger
1 teaspoon ground coriander
1 teaspoon ground cumin
½ teaspoon ground turmeric
½ teaspoon chilli powder, optional
½ teaspoon salt or to taste
1 tablespoon lemon juice
250 g minced lamb
½ cup hot water

½ teaspoon garam masala
2 tablespoons chopped fresh mint or
coriander leaves
12 sheets of frozen spring roll pastry
oil for deep frying

1 Heat oil or ghee in a saucepan and fry half the chopped onion and fresh chilli until soft, then add garlic and half the ginger and continue to fry, stirring, until it starts to brown. Add coriander, cumin, turmeric and chilli power (if used) and fry for a few seconds longer. Add salt and lemon juice.

2 Add meat, and fry over high heat, stirring, constantly, until meat changes colour. Lower heat and add hot water, cover pan and cook until meat is tender and all the liquid has been absorbed — about 25 minutes. Stir frequently towards end of cooking, when mixture is dry.

3 Stir in the garam masala and allow mixture to cool.

4 Mix in the chopped fresh herbs and remaining chopped onion and ginger. (These will be half cooked during the frying of the puffs, giving good texture and extra flavour to the filling.) Cool on a plate for about 10 minutes.

5 Thaw the pastry and carefully peel away 12 sheets. Wrap the remainder and return to freezer. (This pastry keeps well.) Cut each sheet into three equal strips and keep them covered while working or they will dry out. Put 1 teaspoon of cooled filling at one end and fold the strip of pastry over diagonally, then fold again and again, making sure there is a perfect triangle every time. Moisten the end of strip with water or a mixture of beaten egg and flour to seal.

6 When all the puffs are made, heat oil in a deep pan and fry about six at a time on medium high heat, spooning the oil over the tops. Fry for about 1 minute or until golden brown on both sides. Drain on absorbent paper and serve hot with Mint Chutney (page 87).

1 Cut spring roll pastry in three equal strips, separate each sheet as you need it.

2 Put a teaspoon of filling in each corner, fold the strip of pastry over diagonally.

3 Fold pastry again and again forming a triangle every time.

4 Brush each corner with beaten egg and flour to seal.

The quality of the spices used can make a world of difference to a dish. Learn how to assess the spices you purchase and use only as much as is necessary to give the delightful flavours we are trying to achieve. It is better to err on the safe side than drown a dish in too-strong flavour.

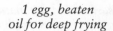

Black Olives With Chillies

A week or two of sitting around in the company of fresh chillies, garlic cloves and sprigs of dried oregano, works wonders with ordinary black olives from a can.

PREPARATION TIME: *10 minutes*
COOKING TIME: *nil*
MAKES *1 jar*

1 can black olives in brine
virgin olive oil
6–8 fresh, hot red chillies
6 cloves garlic, peeled and bruised
4 sprigs dried oregano

1 Drain the olives from the brine and place in a glass jar just large enough to hold them all.
2 Split the chillies and push them down among the olives. Do the same with the garlic and oregano. Fill the jar with olive oil, pouring it in slowly until almost to the top.
3 Cover jar and keep for at least a week before serving the olives. The oil, chillies and garlic can be used again and again for further batches of olives.

Chick Pea Fritters

These resemble the felafel made from brown lentils, but are much nicer when made with chick peas.

PREPARATION TIME: *30 minutes plus 8 hours soaking time*
COOKING TIME: *30 minutes*
MAKES *about 30*

250 g dried chick peas
4 tablespoons cracked wheat
2 teaspoons crushed garlic
2 teaspoons salt
3 tablespoons wholemeal flour
1 teaspoon ground cumin
1 teaspoon ground coriander
½ teaspoon ground black pepper
6 spring onions, finely chopped
3 tablespoons finely chopped fresh coriander
1 tablespoon lemon juice

1 egg, beaten
oil for deep frying

1 Soak the chick peas overnight in lots of water to cover. If time is short, bring them to the boil in a saucepan, turn off heat, cover with lid and leave for 2 hours. Soak the cracked wheat in cold water for 1 hour.
2 Drain the chick peas and grind them in a food processor or mincing machine with the fine screen in position. Drain the cracked wheat, squeezing out as much liquid as possible. Combine with the minced chick peas, then add the garlic, salt, flour, spices, spring onions, fresh coriander, lemon juice and beaten egg. Mix thoroughly until the mixture can be moulded into balls. If it seems too moist, sprinkle in a very little more flour. If it is too dry, add a little more beaten egg. Shape into small balls.
3 Heat oil for deep frying and fry a few balls at a time. Use medium heat so that they are cooked in the centre by the time they are golden brown on the outside. Lift out on a slotted spoon and drain on absorbent paper. Serve warm or at room temperature, either by themselves as hors d'oeuvres or, for a more substantial snack, tucked into pita bread pockets with crisp salad.

Pinto Bean Dip

If pinto beans prove difficult to find, use a can of borlotti beans or red kidney beans.

PREPARATION TIME: *10 minutes*
COOKING TIME: *Nil*
SERVES 6–8

1 x 425 g can pinto beans, drained
½ cup Salsa Cruda (see page 86)
1 clove garlic
2 tablespoons olive oil
1 tablespoon lemon juice
1 teaspoon ground cumin
2 tablespoons finely chopped smoked ham
salt and pepper to taste

1 Mash the beans until smooth or purée in a food processor.
2 Combine with all the other ingredients, taste and season with extra pepper or salt if necessary.

At back: Black Olives with Chillies and Pinto Bean Dip. On the plate: Chick Pea Fritters and Chilli-Cheese slices (page 20)   19

Chilli-Cheese Slices

Mild chillies, sometimes known as banana peppers, are filled with a savoury cheese mixture in which is some finely chopped hot chilli. Serve on plain crackers as a party savoury.

PREPARATION TIME: *15 minutes plus 1 hour in refrigerator*
COOKING TIME: *nil*
MAKES 18–24 *slices, depending on size of chillies*

125 g cream cheese
½ cup finely grated Cheddar cheese
2 teaspoons finely chopped hot red chilli
2 teaspoons finely chopped hot green chilli
3 or 4 well-shaped banana peppers plain biscuits for serving

1 Soften the cream cheese at room temperature and beat until smooth in a bowl or with food processor. Add the grated cheese and chopped red and green chillies and mix well.
2 With a sharp knife cut off the stem end of each banana pepper and remove the central membrane and seeds.
3 Fill with the cream cheese mixture, using the handle of a teaspoon to push the filling into the cavity. Don't worry about getting it right to the end; the tapering tip is too small to make a decent sized slice; but try and pack the cream cheese tightly into the top part of each banana pepper. Chill for about an hour or until the filling is firm.
4 At serving time, cut into thin slices, about 6 mm, using a sharp, serrated knife. Wipe the knife between each cut. Serve as they are, or place each slice on a small cracker biscuit.

Lentil and Rice Pancakes

In South India these are a favourite snack or light meal and are known as dosai. There are two versions, the very large, wafer-thin type known as 'paper dosai', usually only made by professional cooks and often served at breakfast in Indian hotels, and the crêpe-like home-made variety.

PREPARATION TIME: *15 minutes plus overnight soaking and 2–3 hours fermenting period*
COOKING TIME: *about 5 minutes for each pancake*
MAKES *about 18*

1½ cups uncooked rice
¾ cup urad dhal
2 teaspoons salt
1½ teaspoons sugar
2 teaspoons ghee or oil
½ teaspoon black mustard seeds
1 small onion, finely chopped
1 fresh green chilli, seeded and chopped

1 Wash rice and dhal separately and soak each in cold water to cover for at least 8 hours.
2 Drain rice and grind in an electric blender, adding just enough water to facilitate blending. Strain through a fine sieve and discard the rough residue if any. Rinse blender and grind the dhal, adding a little cold water if necessary. This should not need straining as urad dhal blends more easily than rice.
3 Combine dhal and rice and mix well, adding salt and sugar. Cover and leave to ferment in a warm place for 2 or 3 hours.
4 Heat ghee or oil in small saucepan and fry mustard seeds until they begin to pop. Add onion and chilli and fry over low heat, stirring now and then, until the onions start to colour. Remove from heat and cool.
5 Stir onion mixture into the batter. The batter should be of a thick pouring consistency. Thin it down if necessary with a little cold water.
6 Heat a heavy frying pan or pancake pan and grease with a very little ghee or oil. Pour in about ⅓ cup batter, or just enough to cover the base of the pan thinly. The trick is to spread the batter very quickly with the back of the ladle or metal cup used for pouring. Allow to cook on low heat until the bottom is well browned. Turn over and cook other side.
7 Serve with Coconut Chutney made by adding 3 tablespoons desiccated coconut and 2 teaspoons fried black mustard seed to Mint Chutney (page 87), and Dry Potato Curry (page 70).

In 1519 Magellan set out with five ships to circumnavigate the world. One ship and only 18 of the original 230 men returned but they brought back enough nutmeg, mace, cinnamon and sandalwood to make it at least a financial success. The captain of the one remaining vessel was awarded a coat of arms that included two cinnamon sticks, three nutmegs and twelve cloves.

Cheese Sambousek

Little pastry puffs with a cheese filling.

PREPARATION TIME: *1½ hours including chilling time*
COOKING TIME: *15 minutes*
MAKES *about 18*

PASTRY
1½ cups flour
½ teaspoon salt
90 g cold butter
about 2 tablespoons iced water

FILLING
100 g feta cheese
100 g ricotta or cottage cheese
1 x 55 g egg, lightly beaten
½ teaspoon ground pepper
¼ teaspoon chilli powder
½ teaspoon ground cumin
2 teaspoons whole cumin seeds

1 Sift flour and salt together, cut in the butter or rub in lightly with fingertips. Add enough iced water to make a firm dough, handling it just enough to make it form a ball. Wrap and chill 1 hour.
2 Meanwhile, make the filling. Cut the cheese into tiny cubes, or chop roughly. Mix with the egg and ground spices. Heat the whole cumin seeds in a dry pan, shaking or stirring over medium heat just until the seeds are fragrant and dark brown. Turn out at once onto a plate to cool. Mix into the cheese.
3 Roll out the pastry thinly and cut with a medium-size scone cutter into circles. Put a teaspoon of the cheese filling on each, dampen edges, fold over and press pastry edges to seal. Glaze with beaten egg.
4 Preheat oven to hot (200°C), place pastries on lightly greased baking trays and bake for 10–12 minutes or until they are golden. Cool on a wire rack or serve warm. Should be eaten the same day.

Mint and Coconut Chutney, Dry Potato Curry (page 70) with Lentil and Rice Pancakes

Entrées
& First Courses

HERE ARE SMALL SERVINGS with intense flavours — ideal for waking up the appetite. Light eaters may prefer these for a main course.

Chicken Satays (page 27) and Fried Eggplant Salad with Pine Nuts (page 24) 23

Fried Eggplant Salad With Pine Nuts

Ideal for vegetarians and so tempting both in appearance and flavour that even confirmed meat eaters will succumb.

PREPARATION TIME: *10 minutes plus 30 minutes standing time*
COOKING TIME: *10 minutes*
SERVES 4

500 g eggplants
1 teaspoon salt
1 red capsicum
1 yellow capsicum
⅓ cup plus 2 tablespoons olive oil
2 tablespoons pine nuts

DRESSING
4 tablespoons yoghurt
4 tablespoons thick sour cream
½ teaspoon crushed garlic
½ teaspoon salt
½ teaspoon ground cumin
¼ teaspoon white pepper
¼ teaspoon turmeric
good pinch each of ground cinnamon and nutmeg

1 Halve slender eggplants or cut large ones into slices about 2 cm thick, then into strips 2 cm wide. Sprinkle with salt, set aside for 30 minutes, and blot dry on absorbent paper. Cut the capsicums into strips of similar length, but narrower.
2 Heat ⅓ cup oil in a wok or frying pan and fry the eggplant over medium heat until soft and golden brown. Remove to a plate. Heat the remaining 2 tablespoons oil and on high heat stir-fry the capsicum strips for 2 minutes. Lift out capsicum on a slotted spoon.
3 Turn heat low and in the same oil toss the pine nuts for about 1 minute or until golden. Drain.
4 Make the dressing by combining the yoghurt and sour cream in a bowl. Stir in the garlic crushed with salt and all the other ingredients and mix well.
5 Spread some of the dressing on each of four plates and arrange strips of eggplant and capsicum on the dressing. Sprinkle with pine nuts. Serve at room temperature, with crusty bread warm from the oven.

Eggplant and Onion Fritters and Mint Chutney (page 87)

Green peppercorns are the berries of the same plant as black and white pepper but which have been picked before maturing, canned and not dried. Use them in a sauce for steak. Any remaining berries can be stored in a jar in the refrigerator.

Eggplant and Onion Fritters

The batter in which the vegetables are fried makes this a spicy version of tempura. It is important to fry only a few fritters at a time or the temperature of the oil will drop, resulting in tough, oily fritters.

PREPARATION TIME: *20 minutes*
COOKING TIME: *about 30 minutes*
SERVES 6

1 cup self-raising flour
¼ cup cornflour
good pinch of salt
1 cup water
1 tablespoon oil
1 teaspoon crushed garlic
1 teaspoon finely grated fresh ginger
1 teaspoon salt
1 teaspoon garam masala
½ teaspoon chilli powder, optional
500 g eggplants
3 medium onions
oil for deep frying

1 Sift flour, cornflour and salt into a bowl. Add ¾ cup water and the oil, beat well until smooth, then gradually add remaining water. Add garlic, ginger, salt, garam masala, chilli powder and beat well. Batter should be of thin coating consistency. If necessary thin with a few extra drops of water.
2 Do not peel the eggplants but slice thinly and, if large, cut slices into bite-size pieces. Peel the onions and cut in halves lengthways, then cut in thin slices, leaving a bit of the root end on each slice to hold the layers of onion together.
3 Heat oil. Dip pieces of vegetable in the batter, allow any excess batter to drip off, and fry a few at a time in hot oil. Drain on absorbent paper and serve warm with Mint Chutney (page 87) *or* Rouille (page 85).

Kidneys With Juniper Berries

Where kidneys are concerned (or any offal, for that matter) there are some who like them and some who don't. This way of preparing them is particularly tasty.

PREPARATION TIME: *20 minutes*
COOKING TIME: *20 minutes*
SERVES 4

500 g veal or ox kidney
2 tablespoons clarified butter or olive oil
2 tablespoons finely chopped shallots
2 tablespoons gin
2 teaspoons Dijon mustard
½ cup white wine
¼ teaspoon dried thyme
¼ teaspoon dried sage
¼ teaspoon ground black pepper
6 juniper berries, crushed
100 mL cream

1 Wash the kidneys, slice them and remove the core. Sprinkle the slices generously with salt and pepper.
2 Heat clarified butter or oil and gently fry the shallots until soft and golden. Add the kidneys and cook quickly until they change colour. Add gin and flambé, shaking the pan until the flames die down.
3 Remove kidneys to a serving dish. Stir into the pan the mustard, wine, herbs and juniper berries. Simmer for a few minutes, then add the cream, stirring gently. Heat through without boiling and serve with freshly cooked noodles.

Green Peppercorn Pâté

Pungent green peppercorns and sultanas soaked in port are the surprise flavours in this pâté.

PREPARATION TIME: *25 minutes plus soaking time*
COOKING TIME: *1 hour*
SERVES 10

400 g chicken livers
1 cup milk, approximately
3 tablespoons sultanas
3 tablespoons port or Madeira

125 g butter
salt and pepper
1 teaspoon fresh lemon thyme or marjoram
2 teaspoons green peppercorns

1 Wash the chicken livers and drain them. Remove any yellowish spots and cut away the tubes. Put the livers in a shallow dish, pour over enough milk to cover, top with plastic film and refrigerate for a few hours or overnight. Meanwhile, soak sultanas in port.
2 Drain milk from chicken livers. Warm butter over heat until just melted. Put livers in food processor or blender, with salt, pepper and herbs and blend to a smooth purée. Pour in the liquid butter while blending.
3 Pour into an ovenproof dish, then stir through green peppercorns and sultanas with the port. Place dish in a larger pan of hot water and cook in a slow oven (150°C) for an hour, or until top is firm. Cool and chill before serving with toast.

Kidneys with Juniper Berries and Green Peppercorn Pâté

Tacos, Creole Style Barbecued Shrimps and Lebanese Lamb Rolls

Chicken Satays

Chicken grilled on skewers is a great entrée — it's also good for picnics, served with drinks, or rolled in flat breads with salad.

PREPARATION TIME: *30 minutes plus marinating time*
COOKING TIME: *5–8 minutes plus 20 minutes for sauce*
SERVES 6

500 g chicken breast fillets
2 red chillies or ½ teaspoon sambal oelek
2 medium onions, roughly chopped
3 teaspoons finely chopped fresh ginger
2 tablespoons lemon juice
1½ teaspoons salt
3 tablespoons soy sauce
1 teaspoon ground coriander
1 teaspoon ground cumin
2 tablespoons sesame oil
2 tablespoons brown sugar
½ cup canned coconut milk

1 Cut chicken breast into small squares. In container of electric blender put seeded and roughly chopped chillies, onions, ginger, lemon juice, salt and soy sauce. Blend until smooth, pour into a bowl and stir in coriander, cumin, oil and sugar. Add chicken and stir until each piece is well coated with the marinade.
2 Cover and marinate 1 hour, or overnight. There will be a generous amount of marinade because it is also used as the base for a sauce to serve with the satay.
3 Soak bamboo skewers in water for 1–2 hours, then thread each skewer with pieces of chicken, leaving at least half the skewer free at the blunt end.
4 Grill over glowing coals or under a pre-heated grill, about 5 cm from the heat source, for 5–8 minutes or until chicken is crisp and brown. Brush with extra oil during grilling, once on each side.
5 Pour remaining marinade into a small saucepan, add coconut milk and simmer over low heat until smooth and thickened, stirring constantly. Pour into a small bowl and serve with the satay on hot cooked rice, or roll up in pita bread.

Tacos and Tostadas

Taco shells and tortillas are readily available in supermarkets. A tostada is a flat version of a taco, using a tortilla as a base, rather like an open-face sandwich. If you're not too sure about etiquette, the only way to manage a taco or tostada is to hold it in the hand and bite, making sure there is a plate underneath!

PREPARATION TIME: *30 minutes*
COOKING TIME: *45 minutes for beef filling, nil for beans*
SERVES 6–8

6–8 taco shells or corn tortillas
1 quantity Beef Filling or 1 × 450 g can refried beans

GARNISHES
finely shredded lettuce
red tomatoes sliced or diced
grated Cheddar cheese

1 Heat the taco shells in a moderately slow oven for 8 minutes, remove and cool on a wire rack. Prepare the beef filling or heat the refried beans.
2 Spread tostada or fill taco with one or both of the above, then top with tomatoes, shredded lettuce and grated cheese. Serve immediately.

BEEF FILLING
2 tablespoons olive oil
2 medium onions, finely chopped
2 cloves garlic, finely chopped
500 g lean minced beef
1 teaspoon ground cumin
1 teaspoon dried oregano
2 teaspoons paprika
¼ teaspoon black pepper
¼ cup tomato paste
¼ cup water
1 teaspoon salt

1 Heat the oil in a saucepan and fry the onions and garlic over medium heat, stirring frequently, until soft and translucent. Add the beef and fry on high heat, stirring all the time, until beef is no longer pink.
2 Add the spices and fry for a minute longer, then add the tomato paste, water and salt stirred together. Cover and simmer until beef is tender, about 30 minutes, then uncover and cook until liquid is almost all absorbed.

When measuring ground spices, do not pack them down in the spoon measures since this would mean you would end up with quite a bit more than the recipe intends. Especially if the spices are fresh and of good quality (and we certainly hope they are) a little goes a long way.

Onions and garlic have long been known for their healthful properties. When the great pyramid of Cheops was built in approximately 2600–2100 BC it is recorded that the labourers were fed on onions and garlic to keep them healthy and hard working.

Capsicum and Chilli Sorbet

Icy fire/fiery ice — what a contradiction! Serve this brilliantly-coloured, spicy-hot, frozen sorbet to your guests as a refresher between courses and watch their eyes light up.

PREPARATION TIME: *20 minutes*
FREEZING TIME: *about 3 hours*
MAKES *about 8 small serves*

350–400 g red capsicums
2–3 hot red chillies
2 cups water
½ cup sugar
½ teaspoon salt
cucumber slices
capsicum or chillies for garnishing

1 Cut capsicums and chillies in halves and remove all the stems, seeds and white membranes. Chop roughly and place in a blender with water. Purée until smooth. Strain through a fine sieve, pressing hard until only the skins are left behind. Discard skins.
2 Place pulp in a saucepan with the sugar and salt and bring to the boil. Boil for 1 minute, then cool.
3 Pour into small (¼ cup) moulds and freeze until firm. Or freeze in an ice-cream churn, then turn into a bowl, cover top with freezer wrap, and freeze.
4 To serve, dip each mould for a moment or two into warm water, or make small scoops of the sorbet with an ice-cream scoop. Arrange on cucumber slices. If the mixture has been frozen in moulds, leave at room temperature for just a few minutes so that it will yield to a spoon for eating.

1 *Halve capsicums, remove all the stems, seeds and white pith. Halve chillies, remove all seeds and white pith.*

2 *Purée cooked chilli mixture until smooth, push mixture through a fine sieve, pressing hard until only the skins are left behind.*

With the introduction of refrigeration in the Western World the demand for spices to disguise the flavours of food past its prime had fallen right off. With the spreading and mixing of cultures since the Second World War, Asian and Middle Eastern cuisines have become familiar world-wide and the spice trade flourishes once more.

3 *Press freezer wrap over surface of frozen sorbet. Refreeze until required.*

4 *Capsicum and Chilli Sorbet can be served as is, or over sliced cucumbers. Garnish with fresh mint or violets.*

Lebanese Lamb Rolls

Little finger-size rolls of filo pastry wrapped around a savoury lamb filling with pine nuts are served warm and crisp from the oven.

PREPARATION TIME: *45–55 minutes*
COOKING TIME: *1 hour*
MAKES *about 18*

¼ *cup melted ghee or oil*
75 *g pine nuts*
350 *g onions, quartered and sliced*
350 *g minced lamb*
1 *teaspoon salt*
½ *teaspoon ground cinnamon*
1 *teaspoon freshly ground black pepper*
12 *sheets filo pastry*
¼ *cup melted ghee*

1 Heat ghee and brown the pine nuts; remove. Add onions to pan, fry until starting to brown, then add lamb and fry, stirring until brown. Add salt, cinnamon and pepper, cover and cook until lamb is tender, 30–40 minutes. Cool.
2 Preheat oven to moderately hot (190°C).
3 Lay a sheet of filo on a flat surface and fold it over so you have two layers in a rectangle. Place 2 tablespoons of cooled filling on the short end nearest you and roll it up, turning in ends and enclosing the filling completely. You should have a neat roll about 12–15 cm long.
4 Put some melted ghee in a baking dish, just enough to cover base of dish. Place the rolls in rows in the dish and drizzle melted ghee over to moisten top of the pastry rolls.
5 Bake in a moderately hot oven (190°C) until golden. Serve warm. These may be made ahead of time and frozen, and then heated in the oven with foil on the top.

Creole Style Barbecued Shrimps

Having enjoyed this dish at a famous restaurant in the French Quarter of New Orleans, I expressed my appreciation and asked if they would share the recipe. They willingly did. I have made it more suitable for cooking in a home kitchen, but the great flavours remain unaltered.

PREPARATION TIME: *30 minutes*
COOKING TIME: *8 minutes*
SERVES 4

500 *g large raw prawns (jumbo shrimps)*
3 *tablespoons melted butter*
1 *teaspoon ground black pepper*
1½ *teaspoons coarsely cracked black pepper*
2 *tablespoons Creole Seasoning*
(see page 88)
2 *tablespoons Worcestershire sauce*
1 *teaspoon crushed garlic*
2 *tablespoons dry sherry*
½ *cup cream*

1 Remove only the hard portion of the shell covering the prawn head. Split the shell down the curve of the back with kitchen scissors, but do not remove it. Lift out the sandy vein. Rinse and dry the prawns and put them into a bowl.
2 Make a marinade with all the other ingredients except the cream, pour it over the prawns and mix well. Leave for at least 10 minutes, or cover and refrigerate until ready to cook and serve.
3 Heat a heavy frying pan and add the prawns with the marinade, tossing and sautéing until they turn pink. Stir in the cream until the sauce bubbles, and serve with crusty bread. This is finger food, so supply bowls of warm water with a wedge of lemon for freshening up afterwards.

Keep filo pastry covered with a damp tea towel while working or it will dry out and crack when rolled.

Creole Style Barbecued Shrimps

Devilled Crab Soufflés

Even where luscious seafood abounds, crabs are not exactly cheap. Here is how to make a little go a long way.

PREPARATION TIME: *20 minutes*
COOKING TIME: *15 minutes for individual dishes, 25 minutes for one large dish*
SERVES 4

melted butter and dry breadcrumbs for preparing soufflé dishes
185 g crabmeat
1 tablespoon butter
½ cup finely chopped shallots
1 teaspoon finely chopped fresh dill
1 tablespoon cornflour
¾ cup milk
½ teaspoon salt
1 teaspoon dry mustard
1 teaspoon paprika
¼ teaspoon ground cloves
½ teaspoon cayenne pepper
¼ teaspoon black pepper
2 teaspoons Worcestershire sauce
3 eggs, separated

Devilled Crab Soufflé

1 Lightly grease four individual soufflé dishes or one 4-cup soufflé dish, and coat with dry breadcrumbs. Preheat oven to hot (200°C).
2 Flake the crabmeat and discard any bits of bony tissue. Melt the butter in a small pan and cook the shallots on low heat until soft and starting to turn golden. Add the dill. Reserve 2 or 3 tablespoons milk and add the rest to the pan, heating gently.
3 Mix cornflour to a smooth cream with a little of the cold milk and stir in all the spices and seasonings. Add to the heated milk mixture and stir constantly until boiling and thickened. Remove from heat and stir in the beaten egg yolks and crabmeat.
4 In a clean, dry bowl beat the egg whites until stiff and gently fold into the crab mixture. Do not overmix. Divide between individual dishes and bake in a hot oven (200°C) for 15 minutes until puffed and golden, or pour into a large dish and bake for 10 minutes, then reduce heat to moderate (180°C) and continue to bake for a further 20 minutes or until the soufflé is golden brown and well risen. Serve immediately.

Certain spices are not just for flavouring food; they also have medicinal properties. Clove oil, for instance, is the home remedy for toothache — even whole cloves have the ability to relieve toothache while waiting to see the dentist!

Sashimi

This is the famous Japanese dish of raw fish which is served with a dip so hot that it is necessary to warn those who have not tasted it before to go easy on the innocent-looking pale green wasabi horseradish paste. Fish must be impeccably fresh, not frozen.

PREPARATION TIME: *15 minutes*
COOKING TIME: *nil*
SERVES 2

250 g fresh tuna, salmon or other fish in season
2 teaspoons wasabi powder
cold water to mix
2 tablespoons Japanese soy sauce
2 tablespoons dry sherry

1 Remove any skin, bones or fatty tissue from fish, then cut into thin, bite-size slices. Work with an exceedingly sharp stainless knife so that the flesh of the fish is smooth and not ragged.
2 Arrange the slices decoratively on individual plates or a serving plate. Thin slices can be curved into a flower shape, cubes or strips placed in other designs. Decorate with fresh maple leaves or other non-toxic leaves.
3 Mix the wasabi with just enough cold water to form a firm paste. Place half the paste in a small mound in a sauce dish, one for each person. Combine the soy and sherry and pour it into a separate dish, or around the wasabi. The wasabi is mixed into the soy by degrees until the right spiciness is achieved. Each slice or piece of fish is dipped into the mixture and eaten.

Singapore Prawns

This is a quick way to make an incredibly tasty dish of prawns — an invention I have to attribute to my kitchen-addicted husband Reuben, who has quite a reputation as a totally unorthodox but successful cook.

PREPARATION TIME: *25 minutes*
COOKING TIME: *10 minutes*
SERVES 4

500 g raw king prawns
2 tablespoons dried onion flakes
2 tablespoons tomato paste
1 teaspoon crushed garlic
1 teaspoon grated fresh ginger
1 teaspoon turmeric
1 teaspoon paprika
1–2 teaspoons chilli powder
2 teaspoons bottled shrimp sauce
3 tablespoons peanut oil
1 tablespoon sugar
2 tablespoons fish sauce
1 tablespoon dry breadcrumbs
1 teaspoon sesame oil

1 Shell and devein the prawns.
2 Toast the onion flakes in a dry pan over low heat until golden. Cool and crumble finely. Combine with the tomato paste, garlic, ginger, turmeric, paprika, chilli powder and shrimp sauce.
3 In a wok or frying pan heat the oil and fry the combined ingredients on medium heat, stirring constantly, for a few minutes until fragrant.
4 Add the prawns and stir fry until they turn opaque. Do not overcook. Stir in the sugar, fish sauce, breadcrumbs and sesame oil and serve with rice.

Singapore Prawns and Sashimi

GLOSSARY OF SPICES

I am giving the botanical names of the spices so that there is no confusion, since in some instances the common names are misleading.

Allspice (Originally *Pimenta officinalis*. Now called *Pimenta dioica*. Fam. Myrtaceae)
Also known as pimento, this spice is one of very few which are native to the Western hemisphere, the other important contributions to the culinary world being vanilla and chillies (and all kinds of capsicums). The dried unripe berries of a tree that grows prolifically in Jamaica, whole allspice look like large, reddish brown peppercorns. The flavour of allspice is reminiscent of other spices, hence its name. But the predominant flavour is similar to cloves, and like cloves it should be used with discretion. It is used whole in pickling mixes. In ground form it is added to cakes, biscuits and savoury dishes.

Anise *(Pimpinella anisum)*
A seed with a sweet, licorice flavour, used in biscuits and breads. The oil extracted from anise seeds is used in medicine, to disguise bitter flavours, and also in folk medicine because it has a carminative and expectorant action.

Caraway (*Carum carvi*. Fam. Apiaceae)
Perhaps because it belongs to the same botanical family as cumin, caraway is often confused with cumin, especially in Indian cookery books, where it is sometimes listed as an ingredient in curry powder. If you see this, translate caraway to read cumin.

Caraway is a spice that has declined in popularity over the years and you are most likely to taste it in rye bread. It seems to me that the tiny, multicoloured sugar lozenges of my childhood, each one containing a caraway seed, now exist only in memory. In German cooking, however, caraway is still one of the important flavourings and may be found in biscuits, cakes, certain cheeses, sauerkraut, sausages, preserved meats and canned goods. It is also used to flavour the liqueur kümmel.

Cardamom (*Elettaria cardamomum*. Fam. Zingiberaceae)
This fragrant spice is the seed pod of a member of the ginger family. There are two varieties, the large, dark brown cardamom and the small, pale green or creamy variety. I use only the latter variety. It may be purchased as whole pods or in ground form.

Sometimes the whole pods are ground, sometimes only the seeds. Naturally, when the seeds only are ground, the resulting powder is much stronger in flavour, darker in colour and more expensive. Even the outer covering of the pods has a delicate fragrance, so in pilafs and some other recipes, a few bruised pods are used rather than ground cardamom. Purchase it in small quantities and store in an airtight container away from sunlight. I store it in a glass jar in the freezer.

Chillies, Capsicum or Peppers (*Capsicum frutescens* or *Capsicum annum*. Fam. Solanaceae)
Fresh chillies range from mild to very hot. See pages 74, 75 for information on buying, preparing and handling chillies and alternatives to fresh chillies.

Cinnamon (*Cinnamomum zeylanicum*. Fam. Lauraceae)

Allspice

Caraway

Chilli Powder

Anise

Cardamom

Chillies

Cinnamon

True cinnamon is native to Sri Lanka (Ceylon), hence its botanical name which derives from the old Dutch name for that island, Zeylan. Buy cinnamon sticks or quills rather than ground cinnamon, which loses its flavour when stored for long periods. Another reason is that if you look for the fine, pale bark packed layer within layer forming four zeros or five zeros you know you have bought real cinnamon. Cassia, which is Chinese in origin, is a thicker, woodier-looking bark. It is stronger and lacks the delicacy of true cinnamon.

Cloves (*Eugenia aromatica*. Fam. Myrtaceae)
Cloves are the dried flower buds of an evergreen tropical tree native to South-east Asia. They were used in China more than 2000 years ago and were also used by the Romans. Oil of cloves contains phenol, a powerful antiseptic. Use sparingly as cloves tend to overpower other flavours.

Coriander (*Coriandrum sativum*. Fam. Apiaceae)
Coriander seed, dried and ground, is one of the chief spices in curries and is widely used in India, Sri Lanka, Malaysia and Indonesia. The fresh herb is also used but its flavour is totally different from that of the dried seed.

Cumin, Cummin (*Cuminum cyminum*. Fam. Apiaceae)
While both spellings are correct and recognised in the leading dictionaries, they are both pronounced the same, with the 'u' as in 'but'. Cumin is just as important as coriander in curry cooking. It is used ground, but sometimes the whole seeds are nice, sprinkled lightly on bread before baking.

Fennel (*Foeniculum vulgare*. Fam. Rutaceae)
Fennel seeds have a sweet, licorice flavour. They are also used in curries, but in much smaller amounts than coriander or cumin. Anise seeds may be substituted.

Fenugreek (*Trigonella foenum-graecum*. Fam. Fabaceae)
These small, flat, rectangular shaped, pale brown seeds are essential in curries but must be used sparingly because they have a bitter flavour. They are highly prized for health-giving properties. An essential part of Panch Phora. (See page 88)

Galangal (*Alpinia galanga*; *Alpinia officinarum*. Fam. Zingiberaceae)
There are two types of galangal, greater and lesser. The greater is more extensively used in Southeast Asian cooking and has a more delicate flavour. It is a rhizome which looks very much like ginger with a thin brown skin sometimes tipped with pink, and creamy white flesh.

The lesser galangal grows in a bunch of finger-shaped rhizomes and the flesh has an orange red hue. Although it is sometimes referred to as 'aromatic ginger' it cannot be substituted for ginger. It is used only in certain dishes and imparts a pronounced and most individual flavour. Outside Asia it is usually sold sliced and dried. Soak and pound before using, or pulverise the dry spice in a blender.

Ginger (*Zingiber officinale*. Fam. Zingiberaceae)
Available fresh or dried and ground, each form has its special uses and it is important not to try and substitute one for the other. In some recipes I have used both forms to achieve a special flavour. When fresh ginger is young and tender it need only be washed; the skin is so thin it does not need to be removed. But when ginger is mature, the skin can be removed with a vegetable peeler. Grating ginger is a good way to get rid of the fibres found in mature rhizomes.

Mace See *Nutmeg*.

Mustard (*Sinapis alba* (white

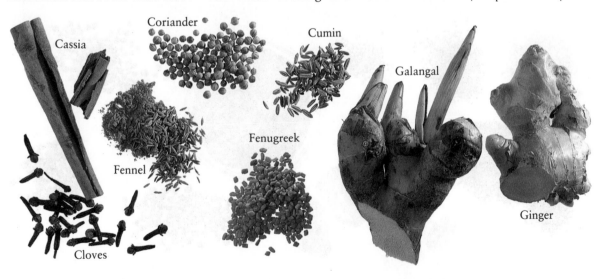

Cassia

Coriander

Cumin

Galangal

Fennel

Fenugreek

Cloves

Ginger

mustard) *Brassica nigra* (black mustard) *Brassica juncea* (brown mustard) Fam. Brassicaceae)
Mustard is one of the ancient spices and has been used not only as a condiment but as a medicine, both internally and externally — mustard plasters were popular for rheumatism. White or yellow mustard and brown mustard, both thought to be indigenous to southern Europe and the Mediterranean, are most widely used.

Mustard is sold in paste form in jars, as a dry powder in tins, or as whole seeds. Whenever it is mentioned in recipes it can be taken for granted that mustard powder is indicated. The paste is usually referred to as 'prepared mustard' or 'made mustard', meaning powdered mustard mixed with a little water and left 10 minutes for the flavour to develop. When a particular blend is preferred you may be asked to use 'Dijon style' or 'German style' (mild blends); English mustard (very hot); 'Pommery type' or 'whole grain mustard'.

Nigella (*Nigella sativa*. Fam. Ranunculaceae)
Now this is a difficult spice to identify because it is known by different names, including black cumin and onion seed. It is not included in Western spice ranges,

but is important in Indian cookery, being one of the essential five seeds in Panch Phora. It is also sprinkled on flat bread, or on special rice dishes such as biriani. The flavour is distinctive, without being overpowering, and very pleasant. Since you would have to purchase it from a store selling Indian spices, I have called it by the name it is known by in India — kalonji.

Nutmeg and Mace (*Myristica fragrans*. Fam. Myristicaceae)
Nutmeg is a great favourite for flavouring custards and other sweets, and in particular for sprinkling over hot drinks. For best results buy whole nutmegs and grate them just before using. These two spices share an entry because they come from the same source. Mace is the lacy aril covering the seed of the nutmeg and whole nutmeg is the kernel of that seed. When the apricot-like fruit splits open, the fresh mace is bright red, but when dried it fades to a pale orange colour. It has a similar flavour to nutmeg but is more delicate.

'Panch Phora' Panch means five in Hindi, and Panch Phora is a combination of five different aromatic seeds used whole to impart a bouquet of flavours to certain Indian dishes. See page 88.

Pepper (*Piper nigrum*. Fam. Piperaceae)
This is true pepper, not the capsicum family which has adopted the name and lists chilli peppers, paprika peppers, cayenne pepper and sweet peppers among its borrowed titles. The small black peppercorns ground freshly over some of the most distinguished plates are the dried berries from a climbing vine which thrives in moist tropical climates and prefers an elevation of not more than 1500 feet.

Black pepper and white pepper are the same berries, processed differently. For black pepper the whole berries are picked while not fully ripe and allowed to dry. For white peppers they are allowed to become almost ripe, then picked and soaked in water for just over a week. Then the softened outer skins are rubbed off and the grey inner core washed and dried until almost white. Because they quickly lose their aroma it is recommended that they be used freshly ground. White pepper is used in sauces and where the speckling of black pepper is not desirable.

Green peppercorns are the same berries, which are not dried, but pickled in brine. Their flavour has a certain pungency, but they are not as hot as when dried.

Mustard

Panch Phora

Nutmeg

Pepper

Nigella

Mace

Saffron (*Crocus sativus*. Fam. Iridaceae)

Saffron, both a spice and a colouring, is obtained by drying the three tiny stigmas from the autumn crocus. It apparently takes around 200,000 of these (culled from 70,000 flowers) to make half a kilo of dried saffron. The work is all done by hand. Talk about labour-intensive — no wonder it is the world's most expensive spice! Ever since I saw a spice merchant carefully count out the tiny precious strands of saffron on a brass scale, weighing them against a small red seed (a standard weight used in the East), I have regarded it as rare and special. When he told me how much the minute quantity would cost, I knew from personal experience that saffron is indeed expensive.

Many years later, when visiting Kashmir, I made a special trip to the foothills of the Himalayas where saffron is grown as a commercial crop. It was too late in the year to see the hills clothed with purple, but not too late to find a few representative blossoms and see the people who gathered the flowers, separated the slender stigmas from the petals and depended on this crop for their living.

It is truly a romantic spice, and its perfume is very special. So little is needed to perfume and colour a dish that it is not really extravagant. What is foolish is to think that one can buy cheap saffron. There is no such thing. The yellow powder that is sold under the name 'saffron yellow' has no connection with spice. As for those large baskets of brilliant orange threads piled high on the streets of some Middle eastern cities and masquerading as saffron, they are usually marigold or safflower. They may offer colour, but none of the flavour and fragrance. Purchase saffron in strands rather than powdered, since there is less chance of adulteration. Store saffron in an airtight container in the freezer and it will keep for years.

Star Anise (*Illicium verum*. Fam. Magnoliaceae)

Although this comes from a different botanical family from anise, the fruits of both contain essential oils and their chemical composition and taste are very similar. Star anise is, however, stronger in flavour. It gets its name from the fact that the seed pods of the fruit open out in the form of a star, usually with eight points. The tree is native to China and this is one of the important spices in five-spice powder. In its whole form, it imparts a distinctive fragrance to certain Chinese dishes. (See Red-cooked Chicken, page 54).

Turmeric (*Curcuma longa*. Fam. Zingiberaceae)

A rhizome of the ginger family, turmeric is the mainstay of Indian curry powders. In both Western and Eastern countries it is usually sold ground in the form of a bright orange-yellow powder. But in some parts of Southeast Asia it is purchased raw and ground to a paste before being added to food. Though sometimes labelled 'Indian Saffron', it should never be confused with true saffron, and one should not be substituted for the other since they have completely different flavours.

Vanilla (*Vanilla planifolia*. Fam. Orchidaceae)

Vanilla beans are the seed pods of an orchid native to America's tropical forests. Together with chocolate they were discovered when the Spanish arrived in America and vanilla has become the most popular flavouring in the Western world. Vanilla is grown in Brazil, Jamaica, the Seychelles, Tanzania, and some of the best comes from Tahiti. It is not really an extravagance because a vanilla pod can be dried and re-used many times. If using vanilla essence do look for pure vanilla.

Turmeric

Star Anise

Saffron

Vanilla

Soups

M OST OF THE SOUPS in this chapter are big soups — not just to start a meal; they can very easily be the entire meal. There are also a couple of very well known light soups such as Szechwan Hot and Sour Soup and the famous Tom Yum Goong of Thailand.

Ham and Three Bean Soup and Singapore Style Prawn Soup (page 38)

Ham and Three Bean Soup

This is a fantastic soup to serve on a cold winter's day or night as it is hearty and thick, a meal in a dish especially if you have hot, crusty bread to serve with it, or croûtons fried crisp in a little oil.

PREPARATION TIME: *10 minutes plus 2 hours soaking time*
COOKING TIME: *2 hours*
SERVES 6

½ cup dried chick peas
½ cup dried lima beans
½ cup dried haricot beans
1 smoked ham hock
½ cup red lentils
1 teaspoon whole black peppercorns
3 large dried chillies
5 whole cloves
2 tablespoons oil
2 onions, sliced
2 teaspoons chopped garlic
1 teaspoon ground turmeric

1 Put the chick peas, lima beans and haricot beans into a saucepan with plenty of water well above the level of the beans. Bring to the boil, boil for 2 minutes, then turn off the heat and let it soak, covered, for 2 hours.
2 In another pan put the ham hock, red lentils, peppercorns, chillies and cloves with sufficient water to come half way up the ham. Bring to the boil.
3 Meanwhile heat the oil and fry the onion and garlic over medium heat until they are soft and golden. Add the turmeric and fry for a few seconds longer. Add to the ham hock and let it cook for 1½ hours, turning it over half-way through and adding more hot water if necessary.
4 When the dried beans have soaked for 2 hours discard the soaking water and put them into a pressure cooker. Add the ham hock and everything in that pan, and water if necessary until the pressure cooker is three quarters full. Bring to pressure, then adjust heat so it cooks under low pressure for 35 minutes. Turn off heat. When pressure drops, open the pan and cut ham off the bone, dicing it into the thick purée of beans. The dried chillies, peppercorns and cloves may be discarded but they will have imparted

their flavour to the soup.

Note: If no pressure cooker is available, simply add the drained soaked beans to the pan with the ham and keep simmering for at least another 2 hours, stirring now and then and ensuring there is sufficient liquid for it not to burn. The finished result should be a creamy smooth purée with some of the beans and chick peas still holding their shape but really soft and tender.

Singapore Style Prawn Soup

In Singapore, if you ordered this, you would call it Laksa Lemak. It is a deliciously spicy soup with noodles, prawns and other extras which make it a light but filling meal. If you are in an area where Vietnamese mint is sold it is worth buying a small bunch for shredding on top of the soup as this is what gives it a distinctive flavour. This herb is called daun kesom or laksa leaves in Singapore.

PREPARATION TIME: *30 minutes*
COOKING TIME: *45 minutes*
SERVES 6

500 g raw king prawns
4 tablespoons peanut oil
2 L water
2 teaspoons salt or to taste
2 onions, finely chopped
2 cloves garlic, crushed
1 teaspoon finely grated lemon rind
1 teaspoon ground coriander
1 teaspoon galangal powder or chopped bottled galangal
½ teaspoon ground turmeric
250 g wheat or rice noodles
1 cup coconut milk
2 teaspoons sugar
¼ cup finely shredded Vietnamese mint
6 squares fried bean curd, sliced
strips of cucumber
sambal olek, optional

1 Wash the prawns, reserve heads and shells and devein.
2 Heat 2 tablespoons of the oil in a saucepan. Add the prawn heads and shells and toss over medium high heat until they turn red. Add water and salt, cover and simmer for 30 minutes. Strain,

Cloves are the dried, unopened flower buds of a tropical evergreen tree and may be used whole or ground. The whole spice makes an attractive decoration when studded in a ham. Cloves are also used to represent the stem and blossom end in marzipan fruits.

The nutmeg tree has either female flowers or male flowers and only the female bears an economic crop. There is a natural preponderance of male trees and this can only be detected after the trees are 6 years old. A nutmeg orchard needs only 1 male tree to supply pollen to 10 female trees.

then discard shells and heads.

3 Heat the remaining 2 tablespoons of oil and fry the onions and garlic until soft and golden. Add lemon rind, coriander, galangal and turmeric, stirring constantly, until mixture is fragrant and brown. Add the strained stock and simmer for 20 minutes. Meanwhile cook the noodles in boiling water until tender, drain and set aside.

4 Just before serving, bring the soup to simmering point again and stir in the coconut milk and sugar. Add prawns and simmer only until they turn pink. Drop the noodles into the soup to heat through.

5 Divide among large bowls. Garnish with the shredded leaves, slices of bean curd and strips of cucumber. Arrange prawns on top and for those who like a hot flavour, serve with sambal oelek.

Leigh's Pumpkin Soup

A chef I much admire who cooks in the French tradition makes a wonderful pumpkin soup and shared his recipe with me.

PREPARATION TIME: *15 minutes*
COOKING TIME: *20 minutes*

SERVES 6

1 tablespoon butter
6 spring onions, finely chopped
1 kg butternut pumpkin
⅛ teaspoon each of ground cardamom,
cinnamon, cloves and nutmeg
3 cups well-flavoured chicken stock
2 cups milk
white pepper and salt
½ cup cream
2 tablespoons finely chopped parsley
small croûtons, for serving

1 Melt butter and fry spring onions over low heat until soft and golden. Peel and dice pumpkin. Add to pan with spices, cover and cook on very low heat for 10 minutes, stirring once or twice. Add stock and cook until pumpkin is tender.

2 Cool until lukewarm, then purée with a blender wand or food processor. Return to pan, add milk, and season with salt and white pepper. Heat until almost boiling.

3 Whip cream until thick and put a spoonful of cream on top of each serving of soup. Sprinkle with parsley and serve with small croûtons.

Leigh's Pumpkin Soup

Bouillabaisse

A big-hearted soup that is a whole meal in one dish. This is the luxury version of bouillabaisse (pronounced boo-ye-base) and it's delicious, but you can use whatever seafood is in season and still enjoy the flavours; after all it is a soup invented in French fishing villages to use up that part of the catch which is not choice enough to sell.

PREPARATION TIME: *1 hour*
COOKING TIME: *20 minutes*
SERVES 6

1 large crab
500 g mussels
500 g large raw prawns
500 g fish steaks
2 tablespoons butter
2 tablespoons olive oil
1 large leek, sliced very finely (white part only)
few celery leaves
4 cloves garlic, finely chopped
salt and freshly ground pepper
4 cups water
1 cup white wine
½ teaspoon saffron strands or ¼ teaspoon powdered saffron

1 Clean the crab. Remove and discard the top shell, the fibrous tissue found under the shell and the stomach bag. Chop the body of the crab into halves, then cut each half in two or three pieces. Leave the legs attached to each piece of body but detach large claws and crack the shells to allow flavours to penetrate.
2 Scrub and beard mussels, discarding any that are not tightly closed. Shell and de-vein the prawns, rinse and drain the fish steaks, watching for any stray scales.
3 Heat the butter and olive oil in a large pan and cook the leek over very gentle heat until just soft. Add celery leaves and garlic and cook for a minute longer, then add salt and pepper and remove from heat. Add water and wine to the saucepan, return to heat and bring to the boil. Dissolve the saffron in some of the liquid and add to pan. Cover and simmer for 10 minutes.
4 Add fish and shellfish to pan with more water if necessary to just cover the

fish. Cover and simmer again for 8 minutes or until all the fish is cooked and the mussels open. Do not overcook. If you like, a teaspoon of tomato paste may be stirred into the stock to improve the colour. Taste for seasoning and add salt and pepper if necessary. Serve hot accompanied by slices of crusty bread.

Thai Hot Prawn Soup

Even the veriest novice in eating Thai food knows and loves (or dreads) the famous Tom Yum Goong. I have had it in Thailand so hot that it terrorises the tonsils. I have also encountered it in reasonably mild mood, but be warned, this soup is for chilli aficionados.

PREPARATION TIME: *30 minutes*
COOKING TIME: *25 minutes*
SERVES 6

500 g medium-sized raw prawns
1 tablespoon peanut oil
2 L water
1 teaspoon salt
2 stems fresh lemon grass or 4 strips lemon rind
4 fresh, frozen or dried kaffir lime leaves
4 slices galangal, fresh or frozen
2 or 3 fresh chillies
2 teaspoons chopped garlic
1–2 tablespoons fish sauce
3 tablespoons lime juice
1 or 2 fresh red chillies, seeded and sliced
3 tablespoons chopped fresh coriander
4 spring onions with green leaves, chopped

1 Shell and de-vein the prawns. Dry the shells and heads on kitchen paper and use them for making the stock. Heat the oil in a saucepan and fry the heads and shells, tossing over high heat, until they turn red. Add the water, salt, 1 stem of lemon grass, lime leaves, galangal, chillies and garlic. Bring to the boil, cover and simmer for 20 minutes. Strain.
2 Return stock to saucepan and add the remaining lemon grass very finely sliced, and the prawns. Simmer only until they change colour, about 3 or 4 minutes. Remove from the heat, add fish sauce and lime juice and serve sprinkled with sliced chilli, fresh coriander and chopped spring onions.

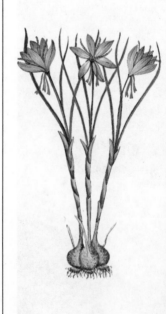

Clockwise from back: Thai Hot Prawn Soup, Szechwan Hot and Sour Soup (page 42) and Bouillabaisse

Provençale Fish Soup

In a picturesque family-run hotel in Nice, France, we had a wonderful meal which started with this fish soup. Served with lots of crusty French bread, it could even be a meal on its own.

PREPARATION TIME: *20 minutes*
COOKING TIME: *1 hour, including making stock*
SERVES 6–8

750 g fillets of white fish
2 tablespoons extra virgin olive oil
1 large leek, white portion only
1 onion
2 large cloves garlic
1 large potato, peeled and sliced
1 bay leaf
few sprigs lemon thyme, tarragon, parsley
salt and white pepper
¼ teaspoon saffron strands
slices of crusty bread
extra garlic cloves
Rouille for serving (page 85)

1 Skin the fish fillets, saving the skins for adding to the stock. Also remove and discard any small bones. Make the stock as described below.
2 Wash the leek thoroughly and slice very thinly. Chop onion and garlic finely, peel and slice the potato.
3 Heat the olive oil in a large saucepan and sauté leek, onion and garlic until soft but not brown. Add the potato, bay leaf, herbs and the strained fish stock, cover and simmer until potato is soft.
4 Add the fish fillets and simmer a further 20 minutes. Season with salt and pepper and allow the soup to cool, then blend in a food processor or use a handheld blender wand to purée the soup. Strain through a fine sieve, pressing through with the curved back of a ladle. Return the purée to the saucepan.
5 In a small dry pan, toast the saffron strands over low heat for a minute or until they become dry and crisp, stirring constantly so they don't burn. Turn out on a plate to cool, and crush them either in a mortar and pestle or with the back of a spoon, then dissolve in a tablespoon of hot water. Stir into the soup.
6 Brush slices of French bread with olive oil and toast in a hot oven until golden and crisp. Rub each slice lightly with a cut clove of garlic, or, as they did at the restaurant in Nice, offer flat cloves of garlic impaled on cocktail sticks so each diner can rub garlic over their toast as liberally or as lightly as they wish. Serve the soup steaming hot, with a bowl of Rouille alongside, to be added to each serving at the table.

FISH STOCK
500 g fish heads and bones
1 teaspoon whole black peppercorns
2 sprigs celery leaves
1 onion, stuck with 3 whole cloves

Put the fish heads, skins and bones into a saucepan with the rest of the ingredients, add 6 cups of cold water and bring to the boil. Cover and simmer for 15–20 minutes, cool and strain.

Szechwan Hot And Sour Soup

In Szechwanese restaurants this soup is served in bowls smaller than those usually used for soup and it is brought on in the middle of a multi-course banquet. It is intended to settle what has gone before and create an appetite for what follows.

PREPARATION TIME: *30 minutes*
COOKING TIME: *30 minutes plus making stock*
SERVES 6

6 cups pork or chicken stock
60 g cellophane noodles
4 dried Chinese mushrooms
½ cup finely diced bamboo shoot
1 teaspoon finely grated fresh ginger
1 tablespoon cornflour
4 tablespoons cold water
1 egg, slightly beaten
1 cup finely chopped cooked pork or chicken
1–2 tablespoons Chinese lemon sauce or tomato sauce
1 tablespoon light soy sauce
½ teaspoon salt or to taste
1 tablespoon vinegar
freshly ground black pepper
few drops chilli oil, optional
2 teaspoons sesame oil
2 spring onions, finely chopped

1 Make stock by simmering pork or chicken bones in water to cover, with a few whole black peppercorns, a few stalks of fresh coriander, a couple of slices of fresh ginger, a sprig of celery leaves and 1 onion. Simmer 45 minutes, add salt.

2 Soak the cellophane noodles in hot water and in a separate bowl soak the dried mushrooms in hot water for 30 minutes. Remove and discard stems and cut the mushroom caps into fine strips.

3 In a saucepan combine the stock, noodles, mushrooms, bamboo shoot and ginger. Simmer for 15 minutes. Stir the cornflour and cold water together and stir into the soup until it boils and becomes clear.

4 Dribble in the beaten egg, stirring rapidly with chopsticks or a fork so it sets in fine shreds. Add the diced meat and heat through.

5 Remove from heat and add remaining ingredients. Taste and correct seasoning so that the soup is quite hot and sour but not overpoweringly so.

Provençale Fish Soup

Main Dishes & Accompaniments

HERE ARE ALL THE FAMILIAR foods you would normally serve — seafood, poultry, meat, vegetables, pasta and grains — but with an exciting difference. The difference is in the spicing. Some dishes are gentle and fragrant, others are full of zing with more adventurous flavour. If a dish appeals to you but you have no liking for pungent spices, just leave out or cut down on the amount of chilli or pepper and enjoy the other flavours. When your main dish is a plain roast or grill, a spicy accompaniment will give the whole meal a lift. Included in this chapter are ideas for cooking grains and vegetables with fragrant and quite gentle spices which make a bland ingredient suddenly come to life.

Couscous and Harissa (page 85)

Couscous

PREPARATION TIME: *35 minutes*
COOKING TIME: *2 hours*
SERVES 6

1 lamb shoulder, boned or 1 kg
forequarter chops
3 tablespoons olive oil
2 onions, peeled and cut in wedges
3 cloves garlic, sliced
2 sticks of cinnamon
¼ teaspoon saffron
2 teaspoons salt
½ teaspoon ground black pepper
2 cups cooked or canned chick peas
2 large carrots cut in 2 cm pieces
500 g pumpkin, peeled and cut in cubes
1 medium sweet potato, peeled and sliced
⅓ cup finely chopped fresh coriander
500 g zucchini, cut in 2cm pieces
½ cup sun-dried seedless raisins
2 cups couscous

1 Trim off excess fat from lamb and cut meat into large cubes. Heat 2 tablespoons olive oil in a large, heavy pan and brown a third of the lamb at a time over high heat, turning the pieces. Remove each batch to a plate as they are done.
2 Add the remaining tablespoon of oil to the pan and fry the onions and garlic until golden brown. Return lamb to saucepan and add enough water to come almost level with meat. Add the cinnamon. Toast the saffron lightly in a dry pan, then crumble to powder with the back of a spoon, and dissolve in a little boiling water. Add to pan with salt, pepper and chick peas.
3 Bring to the boil, then lower heat and simmer for 1½ hours. Add the carrots, pumpkin and sweet potato, fresh coriander and raisins and simmer for 25 minutes or until vegetables are tender, adding zucchini about 10 minutes before end of cooking.
4 Meanwhile, prepare 2 cups couscous as directed on the packet, steaming it in a covered saucepan over low heat about 10 minutes until tender. If you wish, steam it in a fine colander placed over the simmering stew so that the grain may absorb the flavours. To serve, pile the couscous on a large dish, ladle the stew in the centre and serve hot, accompanied by a bowl of Harissa (see page 85).

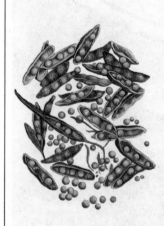

When making mustard, remember that after mixing the mustard powder with cold water, it is essential to leave it for 10 minutes for the flavour to develop.

Pork Fillet With Ginger and Apple

Pork fillet is a nice lean cut and a single fillet is just right for two people.

PREPARATION TIME: *5 minutes*
COOKING TIME: *15 minutes*
SERVES 2

2 tablespoons olive oil
1 tablespoon butter
1 slender pork fillet (about 300 g) cut into
thick medallions
sea salt
1 onion or 6 shallots, finely sliced
1 cooking apple, peeled, cored and sliced
into rings
½ cup unsweetened apple juice
2 teaspoons white vinegar or
1 teaspoon cider vinegar
1 teaspoon honey
⅛ teaspoon ground cloves
⅛ teaspoon white pepper
½ teaspoon prepared English (hot)
mustard
1 tablespoon glacé ginger, sliced

1 Heat half the oil and butter in a heavy frying pan. When it starts to foam, turn heat high and add pork medallions. Cook each side for about a minute, just to seal the meat. Sprinkle with salt, lower heat and cover pan. Cook for 5 minutes or until pork is no longer pink inside. Remove pork and juices to a dish.
2 Heat remaining butter and oil and cook onion or shallots until soft. Add apple slices and apple juice, cover and cook a few minutes until tender.
3 Stir in vinegar, honey, cloves, pepper, mustard and glacé ginger. Allow to bubble and reduce slightly. Return medallions to pan to heat through. Serve at once with steamed broccoli, glazed carrots and mashed root vegetables such as potatoes and parsnips.

Spicy Fried Chicken with Red Devil Sauce

Adjust the pungency of this brilliantly coloured sauce by choosing mild or hot chillies, or sweet or hot chilli sauce. Start with caution and add more if necessary.

PREPARATION TIME: *10 minutes*
COOKING TIME: *40 minutes*
SERVES 6

12 chicken drumsticks
1 teaspoon salt
¼ teaspoon pepper
1 tablespoon ground cumin
2 tablespoons plain flour
4 tablespoons olive oil for frying

1 Place chicken and combined dry ingredients in a plastic bag and shake to coat the chicken.
2 Fry in hot oil until brown all over, reduce heat and cook for 15–20 minutes until cooked through. The time will depend on size of drumsticks.
3 Drain on absorbent paper and keep hot. Spoon sauce onto serving plates, arrange chicken on the sauce and serve with a green vegetable.

SAUCE
2 dark red capsicums
1 tablespoon butter or oil
1 teaspoon crushed garlic

1 onion, finely chopped
2 small red chillies or 2 teaspoons chilli sauce
½ teaspoon sugar
2 tablespoons tomato paste
½ cup white wine
½ cup chicken stock or water
1 teaspoon hot English mustard
½ teaspoon ground white pepper
salt
2 tablespoons cream, optional

1 Cut capsicums in halves and grill until skin is blistered and blackened. Cool in a plastic bag, remove skin and roughly chop the flesh.
2 Heat the butter or oil and on low heat cook the onion and garlic until soft. Add chilli, leaving seeds in if an extra hot sauce is desired. Cook 1 minute more.
3 Add the sugar, tomato paste and capsicum and cook for 2 or 3 minutes longer, stirring. Cool slightly and purée in a blender or food processor, adding the wine, stock, mustard and white pepper. Reheat if necessary and add salt to taste. For a milder tasting, richer sauce (which won't be quite as red), stir in 2 tablespoons of cream.

Spicy Fried Chicken with Red Devil Sauce

Pork Fillet with Drunken Prunes (page 50)

Baked Fish with Fruit and Nut Stuffing

A recipe with a mingling of the flavours of North Africa and the Middle East.

PREPARATION TIME: *15–20 minutes*
COOKING TIME: *25–30 minutes*
SERVES 4–6

2 large fillets of firm white fish, about 300 g each or 1 whole fish, cleaned and scaled

MARINADE
1 teaspoon crushed garlic
½ teaspoon salt
1 teaspoon lime juice
1 teaspoon paprika
1 teaspoon ground cumin
¼ teaspoon chilli powder
1 tablespoon olive oil

1 Combine all the marinade ingredients thoroughly and rub well into fish on both sides of each fillet. Cover and leave for 30 minutes at least, preferably longer, in the refrigerator.

STUFFING
2 tablespoons butter or olive oil
2 tablespoons finely chopped spring onion
¼ cup chopped dried apricots
¼ cup sultanas or chopped raisins
½ cup soft breadcrumbs
½ cup chopped walnuts
¼ teaspoon salt
¼ teaspoon freshly ground black pepper
¼ teaspoon ground cardamom
¼ teaspoon ground cinnamon
¼ teaspoon ground cloves
¼ teaspoon saffron dissolved in 1 tablespoon hot water

2 In melted butter or hot oil cook the onions on low heat until soft. Add the fruits, nuts, breadcrumbs and spices and cook for 3 minutes, mixing well.
3 Place the stuffing on one fish fillet and top with the other or fill the cavity of a whole fish. Transfer to foil large enough to enclose. Bring foil up and fold over to make a parcel.
4 Bake in a moderate oven (180°C), for 25–30 minutes or until opaque when tested with the point of a knife. Serve hot

with rice, Moroccan Carrot Salad (page 69) and a lightly cooked green vegetable.

Pasta with Zucchini and Chilli

I have served this simple vegetarian main dish to my family more than once, and they love it.

PREPARATION TIME: *10 minutes plus 30 minutes standing time*
COOKING TIME: *20 minutes*
SERVES 6

1 kg dark green, medium-sized zucchini
salt
4 tablespoons olive oil
2 teaspoons crushed garlic
1–2 teaspoons finely chopped red chilli, seeds removed
freshly ground pepper and salt
500 g spaghetti or pasta spirals
Parmesan cheese (optional)

1 Wash the zucchini well but do not peel. Cut off stem and blossom ends, and grate the zucchini coarsely either in a food processor or by hand. In a large bowl sprinkle with about 2 teaspoons of salt, mix well and leave aside for 30 minutes to draw out the juices. Drain all the liquid that has come from the zucchini, squeezing out as much as possible. (These deep green juices may be used as part of a vegetable soup stock.)
2 In a large, heavy-based saucepan heat the olive oil and on low heat fry the garlic and chilli, stirring frequently, until soft. Add the zucchini and cook, stirring frequently, until the zucchini is soft but still retains its good green colour.
3 Season to taste with freshly ground pepper and, if necessary, a little sea salt. Move the pan off the heat and keep warm while cooking the pasta.
4 Bring a large pan of lightly salted water to the boil, add the pasta slowly to keep the water boiling, and cook until just tender. Pour into a colander, shaking the colander to allow the water to drain away quickly. Add the pasta to the zucchini mixture and toss gently but thoroughly to combine. Serve at once, with a little freshly grated Parmesan cheese for sprinkling if desired.

Cardamom is commonly available in two varieties, the small green seed pods and the much bigger black cardamom. The green cardamom is considered the best, as it has finer fragrance and sweetness, so it is more expensive . . . ah! but worth it. The white pods sometimes found in bottles are bleached.

Pasta with Zucchini and Chilli, Baked Fish with Fruit and Nut Stuffing

Fenugreek is a bitter spice, but essential in curry powders made commercially. It has a reputation as a cholesterol reducer when taken in the form of a Middle eastern dip known as halba or hilbe. Tea made from infusing crushed or whole seeds is recommended by the herbalist Dorothy Hall as a cleanser for your system. It can also be sprouted and used in salads or sandwiches; though bitter, it has a pleasantly pungent flavour.

Prawn Curry

Depending on the strength of the chilli powder (and strengths vary from one batch to another), this curry could turn out quite hot. Try a tiny bit of chilli on the tip of your finger and assess how much you wish to use. Paprika is used to give the required red colour.

PREPARATION TIME: 30 *minutes*
COOKING TIME: 20 *minutes*
SERVES 6

750 g raw prawns
1 medium onion, finely chopped
2 teaspoons garlic, finely chopped
1 teaspoon finely grated fresh ginger
small stick cinnamon
¼ teaspoon fenugreek seeds
few curry leaves
small stem lemon grass, bruised, or
2 strips lemon rind
½ teaspoon ground turmeric
1–2 teaspoons chilli powder
2 teaspoons paprika
1 teaspoon salt
2 cups coconut milk
good squeeze lemon juice

1 Wash prawns and remove heads but leave shells on. Slit shells and remove sandy vein.
2 Put all ingredients except lemon juice into a saucepan and bring slowly to simmering point. Simmer uncovered for 20 minutes or until onions are soft. Add lemon juice and stir. Taste and add more salt or lemon if required.

Pepper Steak

In restaurants this may be called Steak au Poivre and is always one of the top favourites.

PREPARATION TIME: 10 *minutes plus 1 hour standing time*
COOKING TIME: 5–10 *minutes*
SERVES 4

2 tablespoons whole black peppercorns
4 thick fillet steaks
2 tablespoons butter
salt
¼ cup cognac or brandy

few dashes Worcestershire sauce
½ cup cream

1 Put peppercorns in a plastic bag and crush with a mallet or crack with a mortar and pestle. Don't crush too finely.
2 Trim the steaks. Dip both sides in crushed pepper, pressing the pepper into the meat. Leave the steaks at room temperature for 1 hour.
3 In a heavy frying pan, heat the butter and when it starts to turn golden, put in the steaks and cook over high heat for 1 minute on each side. Lower heat and continue cooking until done as preferred, about 4 minutes for medium rare. Season with salt.
4 In a small saucepan, heat the brandy and ignite. Pour flaming over the steaks and when the flames die down, remove steaks to a hot serving platter. Add sauce and cream to pan juices and stir over heat for 1 minute. Pour over the steaks or serve separately in a warmed sauce boat. Serve immediately with a green salad or cooked vegetables.

Pork Fillet with Drunken Prunes

Pork and prunes is a well-known combination. The addition of spice, port and chilli or redcurrant jelly gives it a new dimension.

PREPARATION TIME: 10 *minutes plus 30 minutes marinating time*
COOKING TIME: 20 *minutes*
SERVES 4–6

150 g pitted prunes
½ cup port
750 g slender pork fillets
1 clove garlic
2 teaspoons allspice
2 tablespoons plain flour
½ teaspoon salt
freshly ground pepper to taste
2 tablespoons butter or oil
½ cup cider or dry white wine
2 tablespoons Chilli Jelly (page 78) or
redcurrant jelly

1 Soak the prunes in port while preparing the meat. Sprinkle allspice over the fillets and rub with the crushed garlic. Allow to stand for at least 30 minutes.

Chilli Crabs

2 Sprinkle flour mixed with salt and pepper over meat to coat each fillet. Heat butter or oil in a heavy frying pan and brown the pork fillets on all sides, turning with a pair of tongs. Reduce heat and cook a further 15 minutes or until almost done, taking care not to overcook.

3 Remove meat to cutting board and deglaze the pan with wine or cider. Add any port which has not been absorbed by the prunes. Melt the jelly in the pan and cook on low heat until syrupy.

4 Cut pork into thick slices and heat gently in the pan juices, together with the prunes, until just warmed through. Do not boil. Serve with steamed baby squash and zucchini.

Chilli Crabs

Visitors to Singapore may have already tasted crabs with chillies, garlic, ginger and tomato sauce, and are smacking their lips at the memory.

PREPARATION TIME: *30 minutes*
COOKING TIME: *10 minutes*
SERVES *4*

2 medium-sized raw crabs
½ cup peanut oil
2 teaspoons finely grated fresh ginger
3 cloves garlic, finely chopped
3 fresh red chillies, seeded and chopped
¼ cup tomato sauce
¼ cup chilli sauce
1 tablespoon sugar
1 tablespoon soy sauce
1 teaspoon salt

1 Wash crabs well, scrubbing away any mossy patches on the shell. Remove the hard top shell, stomach bag and fibrous tissue and with a cleaver chop each crab into 4 pieces.

2 Heat a wok, add oil and when oil is very hot, fry the crab pieces until they change colour, turning them so they cook on all sides. Remove to a plate.

3 Turn heat to low and fry ginger, garlic and chillies, stirring constantly until they are cooked but not brown. Add the sauces, sugar, soy sauce and salt and bring to the boil. Return crabs to the wok and allow to simmer in the sauce for 3 minutes, adding a very little water if the sauce reduces too much. Serve with white rice. Remember to supply finger bowls and large napkins with this dish.

Pepper, the berry of a tropical vine, is green when immature and red or yellow when ripe. Black pepper is obtained by sun-drying the whole berry. Various capsicums are also known as peppers, not because they come from the same vine as peppercorns but because they have also a pungent flavour.

51

Clockwise from top: Mild Lamb Curry, Superb Chicken Curry (page 56), Pumpkin and Bean Curry (page 54)

Mild Lamb Curry

Cinnamon, cardamom and other fragrant spices make wonderful flavours in this mild curry — not all curries are hot.

PREPARATION TIME: *35 minutes*
COOKING TIME: *1 hour 45 minutes*
SERVES 6

1.5 kg boned leg of lamb
2 medium onions
1 tablespoon chopped fresh ginger
2 large cloves of garlic
¼ cup blanched almonds
1 teaspoon mild chilli powder, optional
2 teaspoons ground coriander
1 teaspoon ground cumin
¼ teaspoon ground cinnamon
¼ teaspoon ground cardamom
½ teaspoon saffron strands, optional
2 tablespoons boiling water
1 tablespoon ghee
2 tablespoons oil
2 teaspoons salt
½ cup yoghurt
2 tablespoons chopped fresh coriander
leaves

1 Trim lamb of excess fat and cut into large cubes.
2 Peel onions, slice one finely and set aside. Chop other onion roughly and put into container of electric blender with ginger, garlic, almonds and chilli powder. Add half cup of water to container, cover and blend on high speed for one minute or until all ingredients are ground smoothly. Add all the ground spices and blend a few seconds longer.
3 Put saffron strands into a dry pan and heat gently to make the strands crisp and easy to powder. In a small bowl (or with a mortar and pestle) crush the strands to powder, pour the boiling water over and dissolve.
4 Heat ghee and oil in a large saucepan and when hot put in the sliced onion and fry, stirring frequently with a wooden spoon, until soft and golden. Add the blended mixture and continue to fry, stirring constantly, until it is well cooked and the oil starts to separate out. Wash out the blender with an extra ¼ cup water, add to the pan together with salt and continue to stir and fry until the liquid dries up once more. Add the meat and stir over medium heat until each piece is coated with the spice.
5 Combine saffron and yoghurt, add to pan and stir until mixed through. Reduce heat to low, cover and cook at a gentle simmer for 1 hour or until meat is tender, and gravy thick. Stir occasionally, taking care that the spice mixture does not stick to the base of pan.
6 When lamb is tender, sprinkle with fresh coriander leaves, replace lid and cook for 5 minutes longer. Serve hot with rice.

Scrambled Eggs on Fire

This is typical of the way even a simple dish like scrambled eggs takes on the fiery flavours of India.

PREPARATION TIME: *20 minutes*
COOKING TIME: *10–15 minutes*
SERVES 4–6

6–8 eggs
4 tablespoons milk
¾ teaspoon salt
¼ teaspoon ground black pepper
2 tablespoons butter or ghee
6 spring onions, finely chopped
2–3 fresh red or green chillies, seeded and chopped
1 teaspoon finely grated fresh ginger
⅛ teaspoon ground turmeric
2 tablespoons chopped fresh coriander
leaves
1 ripe tomato, diced, optional
½ teaspoon ground cumin
tomato wedges to garnish
sprig of fresh coriander leaves to garnish

1 Beat eggs until well mixed. Add milk, salt and pepper.
2 Heat butter in a large heavy frying pan and slowly cook onion, chillies and ginger on a low heat until soft. Add turmeric, coriander leaves and tomato, if used, and fry for a minute or two longer.
3 Stir in egg mixture and the ground cumin. Cook over low heat, stirring and lifting the eggs as they begin to set on the base of the pan.
4 Mix and cook until the eggs are of a creamy consistency; they should not be dry. Turn on to a serving plate and garnish with tomato and coriander. Serve with hot crusty bread rolls or toast fingers.

Scrambled Eggs on Fire

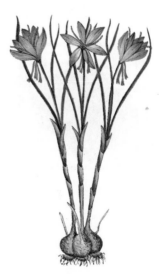

Star anise is a licorice-flavoured spice like aniseed and contains the same essential oil, though it comes from a totally different plant. Star anise is the dried fruit of a tree of the magnolia family from China.

Red-cooked Chicken

A classic Chinese way of cooking, 'red cooking' indicates that the food has been simmered in *dark* soy sauce, which gives it a wonderfully appetising reddish-brown colour. The flavours, however, come from other ingredients, especially star anise. I have used a number of sections rather than whole 'stars', because in many instances the seed pods have been broken in the packaging.

PREPARATION TIME: *10 minutes*
COOKING TIME: *50 minutes plus cooling time*
SERVES 6

1 × 1.5 kg roasting chicken
1½ cups dark soy sauce
1½ cups cold water
¼ cup Chinese wine or dry sherry
5 cm piece fresh ginger, peeled and sliced
10 sections star anise
2 cloves garlic, peeled
1½ tablespoons sugar
2 teaspoons oriental sesame oil

1 Wash the chicken, removing any large slabs of fat around the vent. Cut off tail.
2 Choose a saucepan into which the chicken will just fit so that the liquid covers as much of the bird as possible. Put chicken into saucepan, breast down and add all the ingredients except the sesame oil.
3 Bring slowly to simmering point, cover and simmer very gently for 15 minutes. Turn chicken over with tongs, replace lid and simmer 20 minutes, basting breast with cooking liquid every 5 minutes.
4 Remove pan from heat and leave covered until cool. Lift the chicken from the sauce and brush with the sesame oil for extra flavour. The chicken may be carved in the usual manner but for Chinese style eating it is chopped in two, lengthways with a cleaver, then each half chopped in wide strips and reassembled in the original shape. Serve at room temperature with some of the cooking liquid as a dipping sauce.
Note: The cooking liquid may be frozen and used again and again. It is known as a master sauce.

Ginger is readily available all year round in most large cities, and is best used fresh. If you don't live where the supply is constant and need to store it, immerse the peeled rhizomes in sherry in a jar in the fridge, or better still, wrap it in foil and freeze it, then take it out and grate enough for your use.

Red-cooked Chicken

Pumpkin and Bean Curry

Vegetables which are rather sweet and bland take on new character when prepared in the Indian manner.

PREPARATION TIME: *30 minutes*
COOKING TIME: *30 minutes*
SERVES 6

500 g pumpkin
250 g green beans
2 tablespoons oil
1 large onion, finely chopped
1 teaspoon finely chopped garlic
1 teaspoon black mustard seeds
3 fresh green chillies, seeded and chopped
½ teaspoon ground cumin
½ teaspoon ground turmeric
1 cup coconut milk
1 cup water
1 teaspoon salt

1 Peel pumpkin and cut into large chunks. Top and tail beans and cut into bite-size pieces.
2 Heat oil in a saucepan and gently fry onion, garlic and mustard seeds until onion is soft. Add chillies, ground cumin and turmeric, stir for a few seconds, then add the coconut milk, water and salt. Stir until simmering and add the vegetables. Cook gently, uncovered, until vegetables are tender. Serve with rice.

Beef in Coconut Milk, Indonesian Style

This dish has very distinctive flavours because of its complex spicing, yet is easy to prepare because it just needs to be simmered for hours.

PREPARATION TIME: *30 minutes*
COOKING TIME: *2½ hours*
SERVES 8

1.5 kg chuck, blade or round steak
2 medium onions, roughly chopped
6 cloves garlic
1 tablespoon chopped fresh ginger
6 fresh red chillies, seeded

2 cups coconut milk
1 small stick cinnamon
5 whole cloves
1½ teaspoons salt
1 teaspoon ground turmeric
3 teaspoons chilli powder, or to taste
2 teaspoons ground coriander
1 teaspoon ground laos (galangal)
½ teaspoon ground fennel
6 curry leaves
1 strip lemon grass or 3 strips thinly
peeled lemon rind
2 tablespoons tamarind purée
½ cup hot water
2 teaspoons sugar

1 Cut beef into strips about 2.5 cm wide and 5 cm long and put into a large, heavy-based saucepan.

2 Put onion, garlic, ginger and chillies into blender with half cup of coconut milk. Cover and blend until smooth. Pour into the saucepan and wash out blender with remaining coconut milk.

3 Add all remaining ingredients except tamarind, water and sugar. Mix well and quickly bring to the boil. Reduce heat to moderate.

4 Mix tamarind in water and add. Simmer, uncovered, until gravy is thick, stirring occasionally. Turn heat to low and continue cooking until gravy is almost dry, stirring frequently to ensure mixture does not stick to pan. At end of cooking time, about 2½ hours, add sugar and stir in well for a few minutes. Serve with white rice, a Vegetable Sayur (page 70) and prawn crisps.

Front: Beef in Coconut Milk, Indonesian Style
Back: Vegetable Sayur (page 70)

Superb Chicken Curry

This is one of those dishes which needs a little time and trouble, but the results are infinitely superior to one which is casually thrown together.

PREPARATION TIME: *50 minutes*
COOKING TIME: *1¼ hours*
SERVES *6–8*

1.5 kg roasting chicken or chicken pieces
2 tablespoons ghee
2 tablespoons oil
3 large onions, finely chopped
10 cloves garlic, finely chopped
1½ tablespoons finely chopped fresh ginger
1 teaspoon chilli powder
1 teaspoon ground pepper
1 teaspoon ground turmeric
2 teaspoons ground cumin
2 teaspoons salt
3 large tomatoes, peeled and chopped
4 tablespoons yoghurt
4 tablespoons chopped mint
1 teaspoon ground cardamom
1 stick cinnamon

1 Cut chicken into serving pieces.
2 Heat ghee and oil in a large saucepan and fry onion, garlic and ginger until onion is soft and golden. Add chilli powder, pepper, turmeric, cumin, salt and tomato. Fry, stirring constantly for 5 minutes.
3 Add yoghurt, mint, cardamom and cinnamon stick. Cover and cook over a low heat, stirring occasionally until tomato is cooked to a pulp. (It may be necessary to add a little hot water if mixture becomes too dry and sticks to the pan.)
4 When mixture is thick and smooth, add chicken pieces and stir well to coat them with spice mixture. Cover and cook over a very low heat until chicken is tender, 35–40 minutes. There should be only a little very thick gravy when chicken is done. If necessary, cook uncovered for a few minutes to reduce gravy. Serve with rice, Cucumbers in Yoghurt (page 71) and Seed Mustard Pickle (page 81).

Chilli Con Carne

Mexican chilli powder is a mixture of spices only one of which is chilli so don't use pure chilli powder or the results will be disastrous. If you can't find the Mexican variety, substitute 3 teaspoons ground cumin and 1 teaspoon chilli powder.

PREPARATION TIME: *30 minutes*
COOKING TIME: *1–1¼ hours*
SERVES *6*

500 g blade steak
3 tablespoons oil
1 large onion finely chopped
3 cloves garlic, finely chopped
1 × 800 g can peeled tomatoes
1 teaspoon salt
½ teaspoon ground black pepper
1 tablespoon Mexican-style chilli powder
1 tablespoon paprika
1 teaspoon ground oregano
1 × 7 cm stick cinnamon
5 whole cloves
1 red capsicum, diced
1 green capsicum, diced
1 × 465 g can kidney beans, drained

1 Cut the meat into small (5 mm) dice or ask your butcher for coarsely ground minced beef.
2 Heat oil in a large saucepan and sauté the onion and garlic until soft. Add beef and cook stirring until it is no longer pink. Add tomatoes and their liquid, salt, pepper, Mexican-style chilli powder (or cumin and chilli mixture), paprika, oregano, cinnamon and whole cloves. Cover and simmer 45 minutes.
3 Add diced capsicums and the kidney beans and cook for a further 15–20 minutes. Cooking this dish three or four days before it is needed will only improve its flavour. Reheat gently to simmering point and serve with Chilli Cornbread (page 72).

Turkey Mole

A classic Mexican sauce with an intriguing mixture of chilli and chocolate. Sounds crazy? Well, it's yummy! Substitute chicken or pork if you prefer. Ideal for a party.

PREPARATION TIME: *40 minutes*
COOKING TIME: *about 1½ hours*
SERVES *8–10*

1 × 3.4 kg roasting turkey *or* 2 large
roasting chickens *or* 2 kg pork loin
6 large red dried chillies
2 large onions
4 cloves garlic
½ teaspoon ground allspice
¼ teaspoon anise seeds, ground
125 g blanched almonds, chopped
60 g raisins
500 g ripe tomatoes, peeled, seeded and chopped
90 g butter
3 tablespoons olive oil
40 g dark chocolate
1½ teaspoons salt
60 g sesame seeds

1 Joint the turkey or chickens and use the neck and bony back portions to make a stock, simmering in salted water to cover for 1 hour. Or buy some pork bones for stock if using pork.

2 Put the portions of poultry into a roasting pan, skin side up, and roast in a moderately hot oven (190°C) for 45 minutes or until golden brown. The meat will not be cooked through at this stage. This process runs off the fat and browns the skin. If using pork, roast until three-quarters cooked, about 1½ hours.

3 Meanwhile, tear the dried chillies in pieces, discard the seeds and pour a cup of boiling water over the chillies. Leave to soak for 10 minutes. Put chillies and the soaking liquid, roughly chopped onions and garlic, allspice, anise, almonds, raisins and tomatoes into an electric blender and process to a thick purée.

4 In a large, heavy pan, heat the butter and oil and cook the blended mixture over medium heat, stirring constantly, for 10 minutes. Add 2 cups of the stock and bring to simmering point. Add chopped chocolate and salt and stir until chocolate melts.

5 Place poultry pieces or the pork, cut into thick slices, in this mixture and simmer, covered, for 35 minutes or until completely tender. Make sure all pieces are immersed in the sauce and develop the characteristic rich brown colour.

6 Toast the sesame seeds in a dry pan until golden, shaking the pan frequently to prevent burning. Turn out on to a plate as soon as they are done. Serve up the mole and sprinkle with the toasted sesame seeds. Accompany with hot cooked rice.

Curry leaves are as important for a curry as bay leaves are in French cooking. They are readily available dried, and in some areas fresh. The tree can be grown in cooler climates provided you coddle it through the winter. Curry powder, however, is NOT ground curry leaves. Curry powder is a mixture of spices.

Indian Fried Fish (page 66) and Mixed Vegetables with Coconut (page 59)

Chilli Con Carne (page 56), Turkey Mole (page 57) and Chilli Cornbread (page 72)

Mixed Vegetables with Coconut

A colourful combination of vegetables with very delicate spicing. The fresh chillies can be omitted if preferred.

PREPARATION TIME: *30 minutes*
COOKING TIME: *25 minutes*
SERVES 6–8

About 6 cups mixed vegetables cut into matchstick strips — carrots, French beans, zucchini, pumpkin, capsicum, eggplant, cucumber, etc.
½ cup fresh or frozen green peas
3 tablespoons desiccated coconut
1 cup water
1 teaspoon cumin seeds
1 teaspoon chopped garlic
2 fresh green chillies, seeded
½ cup coconut milk
1½ teaspoons salt
6 curry leaves

1 Cook vegetables in a small amount of boiling water until half tender. Save the cooking water.
2 In a blender put the coconut, 1 cup water, cumin seeds, garlic and chillies. Blend on high speed until the coconut is very finely ground.
3 Put blended mixture into the saucepan with the reserved vegetable stock. Add the coconut milk, salt and curry leaves and bring to the boil. Add the vegetables and simmer uncovered for 5 minutes. Serve with hot rice.

Jamaican Pork

PREPARATION TIME: *20 minutes plus standing time*
COOKING TIME: *40–45 minutes*
MAKES 6–8

750 g pork neck
1 tablespoon dried whole allspice
1 teaspoon crushed garlic
1 onion, roughly chopped
1 or 2 fresh red chillies, sliced
¼ teaspoon ground cinnamon

¼ teaspoon grated nutmeg
½ teaspoon freshly ground pepper
1 teaspoon salt

1 Cut the pork through the thickness of the meat, almost in half, so that it presents a greater surface area. It will cook through more quickly. Place in a large shallow dish.
2 In mortar with a pestle, pound all the other ingredients together to form a rough spice paste, and rub it into the pork thoroughly. Cover with cling film and leave for at least 30 minutes at room temperature, or overnight in the refrigerator for the flavours to penetrate and develop.
3 Grill over low heat for 40–45 minutes or until the pork is cooked and the outer surface is deep brown. Turn with tongs every 10 minutes. Cut the pork into thin slices on the diagonal, slanting the knife at a 45 degree angle so that the slices are larger than they would be if cut straight down. Serve with hot vegetables or salad.

Chilli Beans

A filling vegetarian meal when served with cornbread (try the Chilli Cornbread on page 72) and a mixed salad.

PREPARATION TIME: *15 minutes*
COOKING TIME: *25 minutes*
SERVES 6

2 × 780 g cans kidney beans
2 tablespoons oil
1 large onion, finely chopped
2 cloves garlic, finely chopped
2 teaspoons ground cumin
½ teaspoon chilli powder or to taste
½ cup tomato paste
salt to taste

1 Empty beans into a colander, rinse under the cold tap and drain well.
2 Heat the oil and fry onion and garlic slowly until soft and golden. Add cumin and chilli powder, tomato paste and a cup of water. Bring to the boil, simmer 10 minutes then add beans and simmer a further 10 minutes. Add salt and serve hot. This mixture can also be used as a filling for tacos.

Moroccan Lamb with Dried Fruit served on Fruity Rice Pilaf (page 70)

Moroccan Lamb with Dried Fruit

A leg of lamb, pot-roasted — what's so different about that? It is the starting point for a quite extraordinary meal when spices, fruit and honey are added. Serve with rice.

PREPARATION TIME: *10 minutes*
COOKING TIME: *1½ hours*
SERVES *6–8*

1 × 1.5 kg leg of lamb
3 tablespoons olive oil
2 medium onions, chopped
1½ cups hot water
1 teaspoon ground ginger
1 teaspoon ground coriander
1 teaspoon ground cinnamon
1 teaspoon dried mint
1½ teaspoons salt
¼ teaspoon black pepper
¼ teaspoon saffron strands
200 g pitted prunes
100 g dried apricots
1 tablespoon honey
juice of 1 small orange

1 Ask the butcher to saw through the bone at the bottom end of the leg — this makes it easy to fit the lamb into a saucepan. With a sharp knife trim off all excess fat and the thin membrane covering the meat.

2 Heat the olive oil in a large heavy saucepan and fry the onions, stirring, until softened slightly but not coloured. Move the onions to one side of the pan and brown the leg of lamb on all sides, taking care that the onions do not burn. Add the hot water, and then all the ground spices, the crumbled dried mint, salt and pepper.

3 Toast the saffron strands for a few moments in a small, dry pan — just enough to make them brittle. Powder in a mortar and pestle or between the fingers, and add to liquid in pan. Stir well, cover and cook on low heat for about 1 hour, basting occasionally with the juices.

4 Add prunes and apricots, cover and cook a further 15 minutes or until the lamb is done and the fruits are soft but still holding their shape. Stir in honey and baste meat again. Remove from heat, add orange juice to the spicy sauce, and taste for seasoning. Because of the sweetness it may be necessary to add a little extra salt. Serve with Fruity Rice Pilaf (page 70).

Prawns Vesuvius

Explosive and Italian, how could I resist giving it this name! If you think it's a bit too adventurous, use mild chillies or only the merest hint of the hot variety.

PREPARATION TIME: *35 minutes*
COOKING TIME: *15 minutes*
SERVES 4

250 g pasta (fettuccine or spirals)
300 mL cream
150 g rolled boned ham, cut into shreds
1 teaspoon crushed garlic
½ teaspoon salt
½ teaspoon ground mace
½ cup sliced red capsicum or canned pimiento
2 bird's eye chillies, finely chopped
freshly ground black pepper
500 g raw prawns, shelled and deveined
2 tablespoons finely chopped parsley

1 Cook pasta in plenty of lightly salted boiling water to which a little olive oil has been added to prevent it boiling over or sticking together. Drain as soon as it is tender.
2 Place cream, ham, crushed garlic, salt, mace, pimiento and chillies in a medium saucepan and bring to simmering point. Grind in black pepper.
3 Add cleaned prawns and cook, stirring, until prawns turn white and curl up.
4 Mix in the drained pasta and chopped parsley and stir until pasta is coated with cream. Serve at once.

Seafood Paella

A combination of rice with seafood is only one version of this Spanish dish. But no matter what ingredients are added, one thing always stays the same — the flavour base made from olive oil, garlic and saffron.

PREPARATION TIME: *40 minutes*
COOKING TIME: *35 minutes*
SERVES 6

500 g raw prawns
1 kg mussels
4 tablespoons olive oil

2 large onions, finely chopped
6 cloves garlic, finely chopped
½ teaspoon saffron strands
1 cup peeled tomatoes, chopped
2 teaspoons paprika
2 teaspoons salt
500 g long grain rice
4½ cups fish or chicken stock
2 cooked crabs, cleaned and jointed

1 Wash the prawns and slit with kitchen scissors down the curve of the back so the sandy vein may be removed.
2 Scrub the mussels with a stiff brush, or clean shells with a small knife until they are gleaming clean. Beard the mussels, tugging away the tuft that protrudes from the shell. Discard any mussels not firmly closed. Put them into a pot with a little water and steam for 10 minutes. Discard any which do not open.
3 Heat the olive oil in a large, heavy saucepan and cook the onions and garlic over low heat, stirring occasionally, until they become soft and golden.
4 Toast the saffron strands in a small dry pan over low heat for a minute or until they become crisp, taking care not to burn them. Crush them and dissolve in a tablespoon of hot water, add to the onions and garlic with the tomatoes, salt and paprika. Add the prawns, stir and cook for 5 minutes. Lift out prawns and set aside.
5 Add rice and cook, stirring, for a few minutes, then add the stock and let the mixture come to the boil. Turn the heat very low, cover and cook for 20 minutes. Uncover and push the prawns and mussels into the mass of rice, replace lid and cook for a further 5–10 minutes until the rice is soft and seafood heated through. Garnish with crabs and serve.

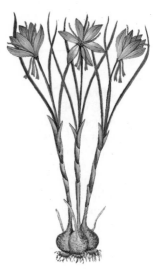

In powdered form, saffron is easily adulterated, and even when buying the strands, you should deal only with reputable shops and people who know their stock. Some of them are not much wiser than the person who walks in to make a purchase. In the old days people were burned at the stake for adulterating saffron but with the removal of this rather extreme punishment, buyer beware!

Thai Chicken Curry

Thai food is certainly hot, but it is also full of fragrance from certain herbs. For anyone who likes spicy, flavourful food, it is worth trying.

PREPARATION TIME: *35 minutes*
COOKING TIME: *20 minutes*
SERVES 4

500 g chicken thigh fillets
4 large red dried chillies
1 onion, chopped
2 teaspoons crushed garlic
1 teaspoon chopped galangal
1 stem lemon grass, chopped or 3 strips lemon zest
2 or 3 roots of coriander herb, well washed
½ teaspoon grated lime rind
1 teaspoon salt
1 teaspoon dried shrimp paste
¼ teaspoon whole peppercorns
1 tablespoon oil
1 cup coconut milk
1 tablespoon fish sauce
1 tablespoon palm or brown sugar
4 Kaffir lime leaves, fresh, frozen or dried
few sprigs fresh basil

1 Cut the chicken into bite-sized pieces. Remove stalks and seeds and soak the chillies in hot water for 15 minutes.
2 Put the drained chillies with some of the soaking water into a blender. Add the onion, garlic, galangal, lemon grass or lemon rind, coriander roots, lime rind, salt, shrimp paste and peppercorns and blend to a smooth purée. If the colour is not red enough, add a teaspoon of paprika.
3 Heat a wok, add 1 tablespoon of oil and fry the purée over medium heat, stirring constantly, until it changes colour and oil appears on the surface.
4 Add the chicken, stir-fry until it changes colour, then stir in the coconut milk, fish sauce, sugar and lime leaves. Simmer until the chicken is tender. Add the basil leaves and serve with freshly cooked rice.

Szechwan Style Chicken

Szechwan province in China is renowned for its hot, spicy food and this is one of my favourite dishes. Of course, you don't have to eat all the dried red chillies, but they do flavour the dish and look impressively menacing!

PREPARATION TIME: *15 minutes*
COOKING TIME: *10 minutes*
SERVES 6

500 g chicken breast fillets
4 tablespoons cornflour
1 teaspoon salt
½ teaspoon five spice powder
½ cup peanut oil
15 dried red chillies
2 teaspoons finely chopped garlic
2 teaspoons finely chopped fresh ginger
6 spring onions, cut in 5 cm lengths

SAUCE
½ cup chicken stock
2 teaspoons sugar
1 tablespoon light soy sauce
½ teaspoon sesame oil
1 teaspoon vinegar
1 tablespoon Chinese wine or dry sherry
extra ¼ teaspoon five spice powder
¼ teaspoon ground black pepper
2 teaspoons cornflour

1 Cut the chicken into bite-sized pieces and coat in a mixture of the cornflour, salt and five spice powder, dusting off excess.
2 Heat the oil in a wok and when very hot add the chicken pieces, a third at a time, and fry on high heat for about 1½ minutes or until chicken is browned, but do not overcook. Lift out each batch with a slotted spoon and drain on absorbent paper. Let oil return to high heat before adding the next batch.
3 After frying chicken, pour off all but 3 tablespoons of the oil. Add chillies, garlic and ginger and stir-fry until garlic and ginger are golden and chillies turn dark. Add the spring onions and toss for a few seconds. Add the sauce ingredients mixed together and bring to the boil, stirring constantly until it boils and thickens.
4 Return chicken to the pan and toss to heat through. Serve immediately with white rice.

FIVE SPICE
POWDER
Essential in Chinese cooking, this is a combination of ground star anise, fennel, cinnamon (or probably cassia) cloves and Szechwan pepper.

Spice and money have been linked through the thousands of years of the spice trade. Wars were fought to keep trade routes closed, lies told to veil the countries of origin, and speculation and bankruptcy accompanied cargoes bought and sold while still on the high seas. Kings taxed the sale of spice and built bridges. Death and poverty as well as great wealth mark the turbulent past of the quite inexpensive seeds and powders we use today.

Back: Szechwan Style Chicken, Front: Thai Chicken Curry

Creole Fried Fish

Pan fried fish never tasted so good as with this Louisiana touch.

PREPARATION TIME: *15 minutes*
COOKING TIME: *6–8 minutes*
SERVES 4

4 fillets or cutlets of firm white fish
2 tablespoons Creole Frying Mix
(page 88)
3–4 tablespoons olive oil for frying

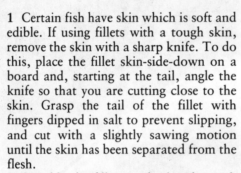

Creole Fried Fish

1 Certain fish have skin which is soft and edible. If using fillets with a tough skin, remove the skin with a sharp knife. To do this, place the fillet skin-side-down on a board and, starting at the tail, angle the knife so that you are cutting close to the skin. Grasp the tail of the fillet with fingers dipped in salt to prevent slipping, and cut with a slightly sawing motion until the skin has been separated from the flesh.

2 Sprinkle the fillets on both sides with the Creole Frying Mix, rubbing it well into the fish and ensuring there is a good coating all over.

3 Heat just enough oil to cover the base of a heavy frying pan and let it get hot enough for a faint smoke to rise from the surface. Sear the fillets on each side over high heat, turning them after the first minute. This seals the fish and gives a good crust.

4 Reduce heat to moderate and cook for about 3 or 4 minutes more, depending on the thickness of the fish. Fish should only be turned once. Lift out on a slotted spoon and serve accompanied by hot cooked rice and green vegetables, or with a salad in summer.

Note: This recipe can be done equally well with chicken breast fillets. In this case, slash through the thickest part of the breast three times, going half-way through, and proceed as above. Do not overcook or the flesh will become dry.

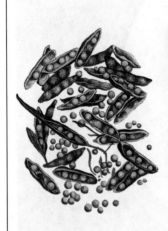

Bastilla

This Moroccan pie was originally made with pigeons, which puts it out of reach of most people. Try it with chicken — it is still very special with its contrasting flavours of salt, sugar and spice, and makes a great party dish and talking point.

PREPARATION TIME: *1 hour*
COOKING TIME: *1½ hours*
SERVES 6–8

FILLING
1 large roasting chicken
1½ teaspoons salt
½ teaspoon freshly ground black pepper
3 tablespoons ghee (clarified butter)
3 tablespoons olive oil
2 medium onions, finely chopped
½ cup chopped fresh coriander
2 tablespoons chopped parsley
1 teaspoon ground ginger
1 teaspoon cayenne pepper
1 teaspoon ground cumin
½ teaspoon ground cinnamon
½ teaspoon ground allspice
½ teaspoon turmeric
¼ teaspoon saffron strands
6 large eggs

PASTRY AND GARNISH
10 sheets filo pastry
90 g unsalted butter, melted
3 teaspoons caster sugar mixed with
¼ teaspoon ground cinnamon
125 g slivered almonds lightly fried in a
little butter
1 egg yolk, beaten with 2 teaspoons water
1 tablespoon icing sugar mixed with
½ teaspoon ground cinnamon
whole blanched almonds for decoration

1 Wash and dry the chicken thoroughly, and joint it. Rub the pieces with salt and pepper and brown in the ghee and oil in a large, heavy frying pan. Remove chicken to a plate.

2 In the same pan cook the onion, stirring frequently, until soft and golden. Add the coriander, parsley and all the ground spices. Toast saffron strands on low heat in a dry pan, crush to powder and dissolve in a tablespoon of boiling water before adding to pan.

3 Return the chicken pieces to the pan, add 2 cups of hot water and simmer, covered, for 20 minutes or until chicken

is almost cooked. Cool, then cut the flesh into bite-size pieces and discard skin and bones. Reduce the liquid in the pan by cooking, uncovered, until there is about 1½ cups left. Skim off fat from the surface.

4 Beat the eggs slightly, then stir into the liquid and cook over low heat until the mixture is creamy and partially set. Taste and add salt and pepper if required.

Assembling the pie

5 Brush a sheet of filo pastry with melted butter and cover with another sheet of pastry. Place on a large baking tray. Repeat with another two sheets of pastry and place them on the first two sheets at right angles. Repeat with another two sheets, placing them at a slight angle and overlapping the first two pairs.

6 Mark a 25 cm circle in the centre and sprinkle with caster sugar and cinnamon, then with the sautéed slivered almonds.

7 Cover with half the egg mixture, arrange chicken pieces over and top with remaining egg.

8 Fold the ends of the filo over the filling, bringing them to the centre. Cover with the remaining four sheets of filo, brushing with butter and putting them together in pairs. Tuck the top layers of pastry under the bottom layers, making a neat round pie.

9 Brush the top with beaten egg yolk and water and bake in a preheated moderate oven (180°C), for 30 minutes. Raise temperature to hot (200°C) and bake for 5 minutes longer, or until the pastry is crisp and golden.

10 Remove from oven, place 2 cm wide strips of greaseproof paper in a criss-cross pattern on top, then sift the icing sugar and cinnamon mixture over. Carefully lift off the paper strips. In each diamond shape place a whole almond which has been oven-roasted or lightly fried. Serve warm, cut in wedges.

2 *Top with half the egg mixture, the chicken and then the remaining egg mixture.*

3 *Fold the ends of filo over filling, top with remaining filo sheets, tuck the top layers under bottom layer making a neat round pie.*

4 *After baking place 2cm wide strips of greaseproof paper in a criss cross pattern over pie, dust with icing sugar and cinnamon.*

Cumin or cummin? Both spellings are allowed according to the Oxford Dictionary, and it is interesting to note that they are both pronounced alike — with the 'u' as in 'but'.

Spices are derived from many different parts of plants — bark, fruit, seeds, flower buds, and even, in the case of saffron, the three tiny, thread-like stigmas of the autumn crocus.

1 *Place brushed sheets of filo pastry at right angles over baking tray, sprinkle with cinnamon, sugar and almonds.*

5 *In each diamond place an almond. Serve Bastilla warm, cut in wedges.*

Lamb Kebabs

A real change from roasts and chops, and quick to cook too, either grilled or barbecued.

PREPARATION TIME: *20 minutes plus marinating time*
COOKING TIME: *8–10 minutes*
SERVES 4–6

1 kg lean boned lamb
1 clove garlic, crushed
1 teaspoon salt
½ teaspoon black pepper
1 teaspoon finely grated fresh ginger
½ teaspoon ground turmeric
1 teaspoon ground coriander
1 teaspoon ground cumin
1 tablespoon lemon juice
1 tablespoon sesame oil
1 tablespoon peanut oil

1 Cut lamb into large cubes and place in a bowl.
2 Combine all other ingredients and mix well. Pour over lamb and stir thoroughly, ensuring all pieces of lamb are coated with the marinade. Cover and refrigerate overnight, if possible, or for at least 3 hours.
3 Thread 4 pieces of lamb on each skewer and cook under a preheated grill or over glowing coals. Cubes of lamb should be crusty brown all over. Serve hot with rice or flat breads.

3 tablespoons oil
2 teaspoons finely chopped garlic
1 teaspoon finely chopped fresh ginger
1 teaspoon ground turmeric
½ teaspoon ground black pepper
1 teaspoon garam masala
½ teaspoon chilli powder, or to taste
1 teaspoon salt or to taste
juice of half a lemon
¼ cup finely chopped fresh mint or coriander

1 Cut the meat off the bone in thin slices. Cut the potatoes in thick slices and slice the onions thinly.
2 Heat the oil in a wok and fry the onions on medium high heat, stirring constantly, until golden brown. Lower heat, add the garlic and ginger and fry for a minute longer or until they too are golden, then add the ground spices and salt. Fry for a few seconds longer, stirring.
3 Add the meat and toss well in the spice mixture. Add potatoes and toss, sprinkle with about 3 or 4 tablespoons of water, cover and cook on low heat until heated through.
4 Lastly, sprinkle with the lemon juice and mix through, and serve garnished with the fresh herbs. Serve with hot steamed rice. A bowl of cucumbers in yoghurt or tomato salad, a sweet chutney and some crisp fried pappadams help transform leftovers into a veritable banquet.

GARLIC. During the reign of King Cyrus of Persia, (559–529 BC) a grocer bought 395,000 bunches of garlic — in one bulk purchase!

Jhal Farazi

This is one of those Anglo-Indian recipes that has come to the rescue of many a housewife wondering how to present the remnants of the roast dinner without having them rejected as leftovers. It is particularly good made with cold roast lamb.

PREPARATION TIME: *30 minutes*
COOKING TIME: *20 minutes*
SERVES 6

500 g (more or less) cold cooked meat
3 cooked potatoes
2 large onions

Indian Fried Fish

Even something as commonplace as fried fish can be given exotic overtones.

PREPARATION TIME: *15 minutes*
COOKING TIME: *5–8 minutes*
SERVES 4

4 fillets or steaks of white fish
2 teaspoons finely grated fresh ginger
1 teaspoon salt
1 teaspoon turmeric
½ teaspoon white pepper

COATING
1 egg, beaten
4 tablespoons chick pea flour or plain flour

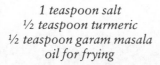
1 teaspoon salt
½ teaspoon turmeric
½ teaspoon garam masala
oil for frying

1 Wash and dry the fish on kitchen paper. Rub on both sides with ginger. Sprinkle evenly with the salt, turmeric and white pepper, rubbing it well into the fish. Set aside for 10 minutes.
2 Dip each piece of fish into beaten egg, then into the flour mixed with the salt, turmeric and garam masala.
3 Heat enough oil to cover the base of a heavy frying pan and fry the fish on medium heat until golden, turn over and fry the other side. Drain on absorbent paper and serve hot with rice, potatoes or a cooked green vegetable.

Thai Green Curry

Those who know Thai food realise that this deceptively mild looking dish can be quite searingly hot, especially if the tiny Thai chillies are used. Use fish, prawns, chicken, beef, pork, duck or vegetables if you are fond of the heat and the flavours.

PREPARATION TIME: *30–40 minutes*
COOKING TIME: *depends on main ingredient used — 10 minutes for fish or chicken fillets, up to 1 hour for beef, pork or duck*
SERVES 4–6

4 hot green chillies
1 small white onion
4 cloves garlic
¼ cup chopped fresh coriander including stems and roots
1 stem lemon grass, thinly sliced
2 teaspoons chopped galangal or
1 teaspoon galangal powder
1 tablespoon oil
1 teaspoon ground coriander
½ teaspoon ground cumin
½ teaspoon ground turmeric
½ teaspoon dried shrimp paste
¼ teaspoon ground black pepper
2 cups coconut milk
750 g raw prawns, deveined, or other ingredient
2 tablespoons fish sauce

Thai Green Fish Curry

2 teaspoons sugar
3 or 4 kaffir lime leaves
¼ cup chopped fresh basil leaves

1 Remove stems and roughly chop the chillies, onion and garlic. Put into electric blender with the coriander, lemon grass, galangal and oil. Blend to a smooth paste, adding a tablespoon of water if necessary to facilitate blending. Add the ground spices and shrimp paste and blend once more.
2 Heat a cup of coconut milk with the blended mixture and cook, stirring, until it boils and smells fragrant, about 5 minutes.
3 Add the prawns or other main ingredient, fish sauce, sugar and lime leaves. Stir in the remaining coconut milk and a cup of water.
4 Simmer until main ingredient is done, then stir in the fresh basil and serve with hot cooked rice.

Moroccan Carrot Salad, Lamb Kebabs and Cucumbers in Yoghurt (page 71)

Moroccan Carrot Salad

If you think you don't like carrots, this warm salad of spicily flavoured carrots will soon change your mind.

PREPARATION TIME: *15 minutes*
COOKING TIME: *5–8 minutes*
SERVES 4–6

500 g mature carrots
2 tablespoons olive oil
1 teaspoon crushed garlic
1 teaspoon ground cumin
1 teaspoon paprika
½ teaspoon white pepper
½ teaspoon salt or to taste
½ teaspoon sugar
1 teaspoon Harissa (page 85) or Sweet
Hot Chilli Sauce (page 78) optional
2 teaspoons rose water or 3 drops rose
essence (optional)
finely chopped parsley or coriander

1 Peel the carrots and slice fairly thick. A fluted cutter gives a decorative effect.
2 Heat the olive oil and on low heat fry the garlic until fragrant but not brown. Add the ground spices and salt, and toss the carrot slices in this mixture until lightly coated.
3 Add ½ cup water and the Harissa or chilli sauce, cover and cook gently until the carrots are tender-crisp. Sprinkle with rose water and chopped herbs just before serving.
Note: If rose essence is more readily available than rose water, dilute 2 or 3 drops in 2 teaspoons of water.

Burghul Pilaf

This would be good served with Moroccan Lamb or Lamb Kebabs, or any meat or poultry dish which needs a grain accompaniment.

PREPARATION TIME: *10 minutes plus
soaking time*
COOKING TIME: *5 minutes*
SERVES 4

1½ cups cracked wheat (burghul)
2 tablespoons olive oil
1 medium onion, finely chopped

1 teaspoon crushed garlic
½ teaspoon turmeric
½ teaspoon dried oregano
¼ teaspoon ground black pepper
¼ teaspoon ground cinnamon
salt to taste
3 tablespoons chopped coriander leaves

1 Soak the cracked wheat in a bowl of lightly salted water to cover. If the wheat is a very coarse grade, it will need to soak for an hour or until just tender when bitten. Finer grades need only 10–15 minutes soaking. Drain, and squeeze out as much water as possible.
2 Heat the oil and fry onions and garlic for a few minutes, until golden. Add turmeric, oregano, pepper, cinnamon and cracked wheat. Stir-fry until hot, but it doesn't actually need any cooking. Sprinkle with salt to taste and serve garnished with fresh coriander.
Note: For a cold dish, let the cracked wheat cool, then mix with 1 large firm tomato, chopped, 1 cup chopped parsley and ½ cup chopped spring onions. Dress with 3 tablespoons lemon juice and 6 tablespoons olive oil whisked together with plenty of freshly ground black pepper and a good seasoning of salt. Toss lightly to mix, and serve cold.

Fresh Pineapple Relish

This is equally nice with half-ripe pineapple or one that is quite ripe and sweet.

PREPARATION TIME: *15 minutes*
COOKING TIME: *nil*
SERVES 4–6

3 cups diced pineapple
salt to taste
½ teaspoon ground cumin
½ teaspoon garam masala
¼ teaspoon chilli powder
1 tablespoon brown sugar
few sprigs fresh mint for garnish

1 With a sharp, stainless knife remove skin and 'eyes' from pineapple. Remove core, dice the fruit and measure 3 cups.
2 Sprinkle the salt, spices and sugar over and toss gently to mix. Cover and let it stand for at least 10 minutes before serving. Serve at room temperature.

Fruity Rice Pilaf

Cumin for its lemony tang and dried fruit for flavour, colour and a complementary sweetness — together they make a rice dish with a Middle Eastern flair.

PREPARATION TIME: *10 minutes*
COOKING TIME: *30–40 minutes*
SERVES 6–8

60 g butter or 2 tablespoons olive oil
2 onions, finely chopped
½ teaspoon crushed garlic
2 teaspoons ground cumin
2 cups long grain rice
½ cup chopped apricots
½ cup sultanas
¼ cup currants
3 cups water
1 teaspoon salt

1 Melt butter and cook onions and garlic for 10 minutes, or until onions are tender.
2 Add rice and ground cumin and stir over low heat for 2 minutes. Add dried fruits, water and salt. Cover and bring to the boil, then simmer on lowest heat without lifting lid for 15 minutes. Uncover and ensure rice is tender and liquid all absorbed. If necessary, cover and cook a further 5 minutes but do not stir.
3 Serve as an accompaniment to meat, poultry and vegetable dishes.

Vegetable Sayur

An Indonesian way of cooking vegetables in coconut milk with spices.

PREPARATION TIME: *30 minutes*
COOKING TIME: *15–20 minutes*
SERVES 6

500 g mixed vegetables or one variety
2 tablespoons peanut oil
1 onion, finely chopped
1 teaspoon crushed garlic
1 teaspoon sambal oelek or 1 fresh red chilli, seeded and chopped
1 teaspoon dried shrimp paste
1 stem fresh lemon grass, very finely sliced or 2 strips lemon rind

1 large ripe tomato
1½ cups coconut milk
2 cups water
1 tablespoon Peanut Sauce (page 86) or peanut butter
salt to taste

1 Slice beans or carrots very thinly, cut cauliflower or broccoli in florets, dice pumpkin or zucchini.
2 Heat oil in a saucepan and fry the onion until soft and golden, then add garlic, chilli and shrimp paste and fry over low heat for 2 minutes, crushing the shrimp paste with the spoon. Add lemon grass or rind and the chopped tomato. Stir and cook until tomato is pulpy.
3 Add coconut milk and water and bring to simmering point with the pan uncovered. Add the vegetables, starting with those that take longest to cook. When done, they should be tender but still fairly crisp. Stir in the Peanut Sauce and salt. If you like, add a squeeze of lime or lemon juice for a more piquant flavour. Serve with rice.

Dry Potato Curry

This is a way of cooking potatoes that I see becoming a favourite even when the meal is not specifically about curries. Be sure to keep the heat very low under the saucepan because only a very little water is used so that the potatoes steam and keep their shape. If you use more water the potatoes become mushy and the result is not the same.

PREPARATION TIME: *20 minutes*
COOKING TIME: *40 minutes*
SERVES 4–6

500 g potatoes
1½ tablespoons oil
1 teaspoon Panch Phora (see page 88)
1 medium onion, finely chopped
2 tablespoons chopped fresh mint or coriander leaves
1 teaspoon ground turmeric
1½ teaspoons salt
½ teaspoon chilli powder
¼ cup hot water
1 teaspoon garam masala
1 tablespoon lemon juice

1 Peel potatoes, cut into quarters, or if

If there's one thing you must know about spices, it is that they are not all the same, even if they are labelled similarly. For instance, chilli powder can be mild, medium or madly hot, and this isn't always indicated on the label. Find out by cautious testing, and write your own label.

very large, into cubes. Heat oil in a saucepan and sprinkle in the Panch Phora. When the seeds start to brown, add onion and fry gently for a few minutes. Add chopped mint, turmeric, salt and chilli powder if used. Add potato, stir well and sprinkle with hot water.

2 Cover saucepan tightly and cook over a very low heat for 20 minutes, shaking pan occasionally to prevent potatoes from sticking. Sprinkle with garam masala and lemon juice, replace lid and cook for a further 10 minutes.

Cucumbers in Yoghurt

This is a sambal that should be made and served fairly promptly as the cucumbers exude liquid. If you want to make it ahead of time, first sprinkle sliced cucumbers with the salt and set aside for about 30 minutes. Squeeze cucumbers to drain off the liquid and mix with the other ingredients without adding any more salt.

PREPARATION TIME: *25 minutes*

COOKING TIME: *nil*
MAKES *3 cups*

2 medium cucumbers
¼ cup dessicated coconut
3 tablespoons hot water
2 fresh green chillies, seeded and chopped
1 scant teaspoon salt
½ teaspoon crushed garlic
½ teaspoon finely grated fresh ginger
1½ cups yoghurt or sour cream
1 teaspoon ghee or oil
1 teaspoon black mustard seeds
½ teaspoon kalonji seeds (see page 10)

1 Peel and dice or slice cucumbers. Sprinkle coconut with hot water and toss lightly with fingers until all the coconut is moistened. Mix cucumbers, coconut, chillies, salt, garlic and ginger into yoghurt or, for a richer, smoother result, use sour cream.

2 Heat ghee in a small pan and fry seeds until they start to pop, then remove from heat and stir into yoghurt mixture. Serve straight away.

Excavations in the Indus Valley of the Indian sub-continent reveal that spices like pepper, cinnamon, turmeric and cardamom have been in use since before 1000 BC when the sacred Ayurvedic texts were formulated.

Stir-fried Vegetables (page 72) and Jhal Farazi (page 66)

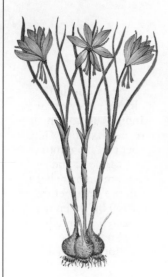

Chilli Cornbread

Not your ordinary cornbread, this one. Jalapeno chillies are Mexican chillies and they have a flavour of their own. You can buy them in cans or, if you can't track them down, use European style chillies in brine, or fresh green hot chillies. Exciting served with Chilli Con Carne, Chilli Beans, Ham and Three-bean Soup, or even by itself as a snack.

PREPARATION TIME: *20 minutes*
COOKING TIME: *35 minutes*
MAKES *1 loaf*

1 small onion, finely chopped
125 g butter, melted
1 cup self-raising flour
1 cup yellow polenta (cornmeal)
1 teaspoon salt
1½ teaspoons baking powder
¼ cup sugar
1 cup milk
1 egg, beaten
2 tablespoons chopped, seeded, canned Jalapeno chillies or fresh green chillies
¼ cup grated Cheddar cheese

1 Preheat oven to moderately hot (190°C).
2 Cook onion in half the butter until soft. Cool.
3 Combine flour, cornmeal, salt, baking powder, sugar and stir well. Mix together milk, egg and remaining butter and add to dry ingredients stirring well. Stir in cooled onion–butter mixture and the chopped chillies.
4 Pour into greased 23 cm square cake tin, scatter cheese evenly over and bake for 35 minutes, or until golden brown.

Stir-fried Vegetables

Vegetables cooked in this way are full of flavour. Cook them until they are just tender but still retain their crispness.

PREPARATION TIME: *20 minutes*
COOKING TIME: *20 minutes*
SERVES *4–6*

2 large carrots
2 cups cauliflower sprigs

If it is only colour which is required for a dish, turmeric (also known as Indian saffron) is perfectly adequate, but nothing else has quite the fragrance of true saffron. That is why I have recommended using saffron strands and only called for them in recipes where the flavour is an intrinsic part of the dish, such as bouillabaisse or paella or a North Indian pilaf or sweet.

---

250 g green beans
6 tablespoons oil
2 teaspoons Panch Phora (see page 88)
1 teaspoon ground turmeric
3 cloves garlic, chopped
1½ teaspoons finely grated fresh ginger
1 teaspoon salt

1 Scrape carrots and cut into matchstick strips. Trim cauliflower into small florets. String beans and cut into diagonal slices.
2 Heat oil in a large frying pan or saucepan, add Panch Phora and turmeric and fry for 1 minute. Add garlic and ginger and continue to fry over a low heat until garlic is golden. Add prepared vegetables and fry, stirring, over moderate heat for about 10 minutes. Add salt, cover and cook for a further 3–4 minutes, or until tender but not overcooked. Serve immediately with rice or flat bread, or as a side dish with fried fish or chicken.

Savoury Saffron Pilaf

Well-flavoured rice cooked in stock with spices. With its garnish of peas, nuts and eggs, it could be a meal in itself.

PREPARATION TIME: *20 minutes plus time for draining rice*
COOKING TIME: *45 minutes plus 2 hours for stock*
SERVES *4–6*

1 kg chicken soup pieces or 3 lamb shanks
4 cardamom pods
10 whole black peppercorns
4½ teaspoons salt
1 onion
3 whole cloves
2½ cups long grain rice
1 tablespoon ghee
2 tablespoons oil
1 large onion, finely sliced
2 cloves garlic, crushed
½ teaspoon finely grated fresh ginger
¼ teaspoon saffron strands
½ teaspoon garam masala
½ teaspoon ground cardamom
3 tablespoons rose water
¼ cup sultanas
¼ cup slivered almonds, fried in ghee or oil
1 cup hot cooked green peas
3 hard-boiled eggs, halved

Savoury Saffron Pilaf

1 Make a strong, well-flavoured stock by simmering chicken or lamb in water to cover with cardamom pods, peppercorns, 2 teaspoons salt and the onion stuck with cloves. Simmer about 2 hours. Strain stock and measure 4 cups.

2 Wash rice well in several changes of cold water and drain in a colander for at least 1 hour.

3 Heat ghee in a large saucepan and fry sliced onion until golden. Add garlic and ginger and fry for 1 minute, stirring constantly. Add rice and fry 5 minutes longer over a moderate heat, stirring with a slotted metal spoon. (A slotted spoon does not break the long delicate grains of rice

which add so much to the appearance of this dish.)

4 Add hot stock, saffron, garam masala, cardamom, remaining salt, rose water and sultanas and stir well. Cover pan with a tightly fitting lid and cook over a very low heat for 20 minutes. Do not uncover saucepan or stir rice during cooking time.

5 Remove rice from heat, uncover and let steam escape for 5 minutes. Fluff up rice gently with a fork and place in a dish, again using a slotted metal spoon. Garnish with almonds, peas and eggs and serve hot accompanied by curries, chutneys, cucumbers in sour cream or yoghurt, and crisp fried pappadams.

CHILLIES & HOW TO HANDLE THEM

There are said to be over ninety varieties of chillies. All belong to the botanical genus *Capsicum*. We show you some of the more readily available kinds, those that are grown commercially, and tell you how much heat you can expect from them.

Whichever type of hot chilli you use, it is wise to protect yourself by wearing gloves when seeding or chopping them. They contain capsaicin, a substance which is extremely pungent and can cause considerable discomfort if allowed to come in contact with the skin. Capsaicin is concentrated mainly in the central membrane and seeds, but is also present in the flesh. The tiny, thin-skinned chillies have the highest capsaicin content, and should be handled (and consumed) with caution.

If you're reading this AFTER having a close encounter of the torrid kind with chillies and your hands are on fire, try applying a paste of bicarbonate of soda. Apparently the alkali neutralises to some extent the effect of the capsaicin. Above all, if you've been indiscreet handling chillies, keep your hands away from your eyes, and don't touch children.

You don't have to suffer to enjoy the flavour of chillies. There are some mild varieties which will cause no discomfort. The larger and rounder in shape they are, the safer you are. In some countries they are called capsicums, and in others may be known as sweet peppers or bell peppers.

Where fresh chillies are used and a mild flavouring is required simply wash the chilli and add whole, while the dish is simmering. Lift out the chilli and discard it before serving.

For those who are seeking the hot quality to give zip to a particular dish or sauce, look for small chillies or thin, long ones. The hottest of all are the tiny bird's-eye chillies.

Chopping Chillies — the easiest way

When thin slices of chilli are required, it is safer to use sharp kitchen scissors. Hold the chilli by its stem and snip from the far end. Take care when chopping chillies for those fiery hot dishes! Cover your hands with close fitting plastic gloves (loose fitting gloves are clumsy and difficult to work with). If you have no gloves try not to touch the cut surfaces — it can be done by holding the chilli by its stem. But afterwards, always wash your hands with soap and hot water two or three times. Chillies can be so hot that the tingling hotness can linger for hours.

Reducing the Heat

Remove stalk of chilli and make a slit down the side to remove the seeds, scraping them out with the tip of a small sharp knife. *Or* cut the chilli in half lengthwise and remove the central membrane together with the seeds.

Easy Ways to Buy Chillies

You can, of course, add that dash of pungency and heat to a dish without ever handling fresh chillies. One way is to use hot pepper sauce or chilli sauce — certainly convenient. Or you can buy chopped chillies in bottles, or what is called sambal olek, an Indonesian sambal which is nothing more than hot chillies ground up, seeds and all, with salt and probably some preservative. Spooning it out of a jar is quicker and safer than chopping the chillies yourself.

In Chinese or other Asian cuisines you may use chilli bean sauce or, as the label on the jar says, 'Sauce de Soja au Piment'. It is a mixture of hot chillies and fermented soy beans ground up in an oil base. It does have good flavour, but beware — it is also extremely hot.

Another Chinese invention is chilli oil — purchase it in small bottles and put just a drop or two into a dish at the end of cooking if you wish to add a chilli flavour and considerable heat.

1 It is wise to protect your hands with plastic gloves while chopping or slicing chillies.

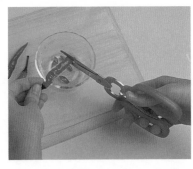

2 To slice chillies thinly use kitchen scissors. Hold the chilli by its stem and snip from the other end.

1 To prepare chilli flowers use scissors to snip off the end of the chilli.

2 Cut thin strips of chilli working from the base to the stem. Place the chilli in cold water, cover and refrigerate overnight.

Chutneys, Pickles & Marinades

THIS IS A BRANCH OF cookery that really depends on spices. What would chutneys and pickles be without the flavours that come from spices — only sweet, sour and salty, with none of the sparkle. In addition to cooked chutneys of the Major Grey school, which keep for long periods, you will find some fresh chutneys which should be used within a day or two. Also in this chapter are marinades and sauces which are not tied to just one recipe, but are quite versatile.

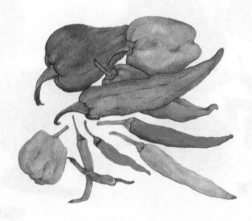

Clockwise from back: Chilli Jelly, Sweet Hot Chilli Sauce with Spring Rolls (page 78),
Pineapple Chutney (page 84), Whole-seed Mustard, French Style (page 78)

Chilli Jelly

Not really as lethal as it sounds or as hot as it looks! Most of the colour comes from sweet peppers or capsicums, but a hint of chilli makes this an exciting alternative to cranberry or mint jelly. The brilliant vermilion colour makes a statement on the plate even before you find out how wonderfully it complements roast turkey, ham or other meats. Serve a small scoop in half a lime or lemon shell, or in the hollow of a peach.

PREPARATION TIME: *20 minutes*
COOKING TIME: *15 minutes*
MAKES *3 cups*

500 g bright red capsicums
3 or 4 hot red chillies
1–2 cloves garlic
1 large onion, peeled and
quartered
1 cup water
1 cup white wine vinegar
1½ teaspoons salt
2 cups sugar
1 × 50 g packet powdered pectin

1 Wash the capsicums well. Cut in halves lengthways and discard all the central membrane, seeds and stems. Cut the capsicums into pieces. Stem and seed the chillies too, wearing gloves, as hot chillies can cause much discomfort.
2 Put capsicums and chillies into a blender with the garlic, onion and water, and blend to a smooth purée. If the blender jar is not large, do this in two lots. Empty into a fine nylon sieve over a bowl, and press hard with a spoon to extract as much juice and purée as possible. Discard the particles of tough skin left in the sieve. There should be about 3 cups of purée.
3 Put the purée and juice, vinegar, salt and sugar into a heavy stainless saucepan and bring to a rolling boil, stirring until sugar dissolves. Lower the heat and sprinkle the pectin over the liquid, then return to a fast boil and boil for 5 minutes, stirring frequently. Pour into sterilised jars and leave to cool and set, then cover airtight.
Note: If fresh red chillies are out of season, use a tablespoon of Sweet Chilli Sauce (page 78), or some bought chilli sauce.

Jars must be thoroughly clean and sterile. Immerse them in water in a large saucepan, bring to the boil and boil for 10 minutes, *or* put jars filled with boiling water into the microwave and cook on the highest setting for 6 minutes. Alternatively, put the well-washed jars on a tray in a moderately slow oven for at least 20 minutes. Handle them with an oven mitt and use jars while hot.

Sweet Hot Chilli Sauce

This is not really as sweet and mild as the American-style bottled sauce that bears the same name. It has more bite. Knowing your own heat tolerance and that of your guests is important. Choose your flavour accents accordingly.

PREPARATION TIME: *10 minutes*
COOKING TIME: *1 hour*
MAKES *about 3 cups*

250 g fresh red chillies or ½ cup chilli
powder
3 cups white vinegar
250 g sultanas
2 tablespoons finely grated fresh ginger
6–8 cloves garlic, peeled
3 teaspoons salt
3 cups sugar

1 If using fresh chillies, put on gloves before removing stems and seeds. Put them into a stainless steel or enamel saucepan with the vinegar, the sultanas, the ginger and the garlic crushed with salt.
2 Bring to the boil and simmer gently until the sultanas are soft. Add the sugar, stir until dissolved and cook about 15 minutes longer. Cool, then purée in a blender or push through a sieve. Pour into sterilised bottles and seal. Keeps well.
Note: If this sauce is still too pungent for your taste, mix it with bottled or homemade tomato sauce until you have the degree of hotness that's right for you.

Whole-Seed Mustard, French Style

A lovely gift at Christmas. Start saving nice-looking jars or pots as containers.

PREPARATION TIME: *20 minutes plus*
soaking time
COOKING TIME: *nil*
MAKES *4 small jars*

1 cup whole yellow mustard seeds
1 cup whole black mustard seeds
1 bay leaf
white wine vinegar

dry white wine
3 tablespoons honey
1 teaspoon dried tarragon
1 teaspoon crushed garlic (optional)

1 Place yellow and black mustard seeds in a glass bowl with bay leaf. Cover with white wine vinegar, place a plate on top and leave to soak overnight.
2 Next day remove the bay leaf and blend half of the soaked mustard seeds in a blender or food processor until smooth, adding enough dry white wine to keep the mixture moving.
3 Combine the blended mustard with the remaining soaked mustard seeds and sweeten to taste with honey. Stir in tarragon and garlic and add enough extra white wine to achieve a spreading consistency.
4 Spoon into sterilised jars and seal with tight-fitting plastic-lined lids. Place in a dark cupboard to mature.

Scandinavian Mustard Sauce

This is a mild and sweet flavoured sauce ideal for serving with smoked fish, cold meats, or as a dressing over hot cooked vegetables such as new potatoes or broccoli. Be careful when adding the oil, that you do it very slowly. Like mayonnaise, this sauce will curdle if you add too much oil at a time.

PREPARATION TIME: *10 minutes*
COOKING TIME: *nil*
MAKES *about 1 cup*

⅓ cup prepared seed mustard, French style
2 teaspoons dry mustard powder
2 tablespoons sugar
2 tablespoons red or white wine vinegar
½ cup olive oil
¼ cup chopped fresh dill weed

1 Combine the seed mustard, powdered mustard and sugar in a bowl. Stir in the vinegar.
2 Add the oil very gradually, whisking as for mayonnaise. The sauce will thicken as the oil is added. Mix in the dill. It may be kept for a few days in the refrigerator; add the dill just before serving.

White mustard as it is called, though it is actually pale yellow, is a strong preservative which is why it is often used in pickling recipes.
There are two other types of mustard seed, black and brown. The black is hottest, the brown less so and the white, or yellow, the most mild. White mustard is mixed with turmeric to make English and American mustards.

Scandinavian Mustard Sauce with smoked salmon salad

Lemon and Date Chutney and Sweet Mango Chutney (page 83)

Lemon and Date Chutney

One of my favourite chutneys to serve with rice and curry meals — or to spread on cold meat sandwiches or serve as a relish with fried fish, roast meats or poultry.

PREPARATION TIME: *40 minutes plus soaking time*
COOKING TIME: *35 minutes*
MAKES *about 6 cups*

500 g dates
6 salted lemons or limes (see note below)
10–15 large dried red chillies
1 tablespoon black mustard seed
2–3 cups white vinegar
20 cloves garlic, peeled
2 tablespoons finely grated fresh ginger
3 cups sugar
1 cup sultanas

1 Remove seeds from the dates and cut dates in halves or quarters. Cut the salted lemons or limes into fine strips.
2 Discard stems of chillies, break each chilli in halves and shake the seeds out. Put chillies and mustard seeds into a glass or china bowl and soak in vinegar overnight.
3 Next day, grind in an electric blender with garlic and ginger. In a non-aluminium saucepan put blended ingredients and sugar. Stir and bring to the boil. Add the dates, lemons and sultanas and bring back to the boil. Add extra vinegar if the mixture seems too thick. Turn heat low and simmer, stirring frequently, for about 20 minutes longer. Put into clean, hot jars with non-metal lids.
Note: Salted lemons or limes are easy enough to make, they just take time to mature. Wash and dry the fruit, slit each one twice, not separating the pieces, and stuff with coarse salt. Pack into a stone or glass jar and cover tightly with non-metal lids. Leave in the sun every day for 3 weeks, then store in a cupboard until they turn brown and soft before using. They will keep for years. Another way is to drop lemon or lime skins into a bottle of salted vinegar as you use them. Use a glass-stoppered jar and when the jar is almost full, leave it in a cupboard for at least a month, when it will be ready.

Seed Mustard Pickle

This is a favourite relish in many Asian countries — crunchy pickled vegetables in a seed mustard sauce — a welcome change to serve as a relish with cold meats or as an accompaniment to curry and rice.

PREPARATION TIME: *1 hour plus soaking time*
COOKING TIME: *about 30 minutes*
MAKES *1 jar*

½ cup black mustard seeds
3 cups vinegar
2 teaspoons salt
1 teaspoon ground turmeric
1 cup peeled shallots or tiny pickling onions
12 fresh red or green chilllies
1 cup green beans, sliced
1 cup cauliflower florets
1 cup carrot matchstick strips
6 cloves garlic
1 tablespoon grated fresh ginger
3 teaspoons sugar

1 Soak mustard seeds in vinegar to cover overnight.
2 Next day bring remaining vinegar to the boil with salt and turmeric in a medium-sized enamel saucepan. Put onions in, bring to the boil and boil for 1 minute. Lift out on slotted spoon and put into a nylon strainer to drain and cool. Do the same with chillies and the other vegetables. Allow extra time for the beans, carrots and cauliflower which should be tender but still crisp to bite.
3 When all the vegetables are drained and cooled, put them into a clean dry bottle or earthenware jar.
4 In electric blender, purée the soaked mustard with the garlic, ginger and sugar. Mix in vinegar remaining in pan and pour over the vegetables in the bottle, adding more vinegar if necessary to cover vegetables. Use a jar with a glass lid or cork stopper if possible. If jar has a metal lid, cover with two thicknesses of greaseproof paper first. This pickle will keep for months.

Seed Mustard Pickle with stir-fried vegetables

One of the commonest of spices, mustard is so much part of the kitchen that we often take it for granted. Before the exotic spices became widely available, old-fashioned meals were brought to savoury perfection by adding a touch of mustard. To help you recall, how about a teaspoon of made mustard in the gravy for bangers and mash? Or a tablespoon of mild whole-grain mustard or Dijon mustard, in the sauce for fish or chicken?

If storage jars have metal lids, put a double fold of plastic freezer wrap or wax paper under the lid so that the vinegar cannot corrode the metal.

Turmeric is of the ginger family and is made from the rhizomes, which are first boiled, then dried, polished and ground. It has a distinctive pungent taste and is used both as a flavouring and as a dye. It is present in rice and curries in the East, and margarine, butter, cheese and fruit drinks in the West!

Italian-style Pickled Chillies

Chilli and Apple Relish

PREPARATION TIME: *5 minutes*
COOKING TIME: *1 hour*
MAKES *2 cups*

6 red chillies, seeded and finely sliced
500 g red capsicums, finely diced
1 large onion, finely diced
1 large green apple, peeled and grated
2 teaspoons finely chopped garlic
3 teaspoons finely chopped fresh ginger
1½ cups sugar
1½ cups white vinegar

1 For ease and speed, all the ingredients except vinegar and sugar may be roughly chopped and placed in a food processor for fine chopping.
2 Place in a non-aluminium saucepan with the vinegar and sugar and simmer 1 hour or until thick, stirring frequently. Cooking time will depend on size of the saucepan — a wide pan makes for quicker evaporation.
3 Have ready washed and sterilised glass jars with non-metal lids. Pour into hot jars and seal while hot.

Italian-style Pickled Chillies

When those long, bright red, not-too-hot chillies are in season pickle some of them in this simple way and have them on hand for adding to pasta and other dishes.

PREPARATION TIME: *10 minutes*
COOKING TIME: *15 minutes*
MAKES *1 jar*

500 g red chillies
1 cup white vinegar
1 cup water
1 teaspoon salt
10 cloves garlic, peeled and split
olive oil

1 Wash the chillies, and with kitchen scissors snip off the stems. Cut the chillies into pieces.
2 In a stainless saucepan bring the vinegar, water and salt to the boil and drop in about a cup of chillies at a time. Let them return to the boil, cook 1 minute,

then lift out on a slotted spoon and put into a bowl.
3 When all have been blanched, leave them to cool, then pack into a large glass jar with cloves of garlic tucked in here and there. Add olive oil to fill, letting it trickle in slowly so that there are no air spaces. Leave for at least a week before using, and when the level of oil drops in the jar, replace with more oil so that the chillies are always immersed.

Spiced Prunes

PREPARATION TIME: *15 minutes*
COOKING TIME: *7–10 minutes*
MAKES *1 jar*

500 g dessert prunes
1 cup white or red wine vinegar
1 cup water
½ cup sugar
1 stick cinnamon
3 cloves
10 whole allspice

1 Pack prunes into clean jars with non-metal lids.
2 Put vinegar and water into a stainless steel or ceramic pan with the sugar and spices and bring to the boil. Simmer for five minutes, then allow to cool.
3 Pour cool vinegar mixture over the prunes until they are immersed. Cover tightly and keep at least a week before eating.
Note: If jars have metal lids, put a double fold of plastic freezer wrap or even wax paper under the lid so that the vinegar cannot corrode the metal.

Tomato and Chilli Relish

A new version of a tried and true favourite for more adventurous tastebuds.

PREPARATION TIME: *30–45 minutes plus standing time*
COOKING TIME: *about 2 hours*
MAKES *10–12 cups*

3 kg ripe red tomatoes
1 kg onions

3 tablespoons salt
6 red chillies (or to taste)
750 g sugar
900 mL brown vinegar
¾ cup plain flour
1 tablespoon mustard
1 tablespoon curry powder
1 tablespoon turmeric

1 Peel and dice tomatoes and onions, sprinkle with salt and leave overnight in a non-metal bowl.
2 Drain well and simmer with the seeded and chopped chillies in a non-aluminium saucepan for 45 minutes.
3 Combine sugar, flour, mustard, curry powder and turmeric with enough vinegar to make a paste. Add the remaining vinegar to tomatoes, onions and chillies.
4 Stir in blended ingredients, boil and stir until thick. Turn heat low and simmer for 1 hour, stirring from time to time to prevent sticking.
5 Bottle while hot in heated jars. Label when cold.

Corn Relish

A new and spicier version, quick and easy to make.

PREPARATION TIME: *20 minutes*
COOKING TIME: *40 minutes*
MAKES *about 6 cups*

1 large can whole kernel corn
1 large white onion, chopped
1 large green capsicum seeded and chopped
1 large red capsicum seeded and chopped
3 red chillies, chopped
1 teaspoon crushed garlic
2 teaspoons yellow mustard seeds
2 teaspoons celery seed
750 mL white vinegar
2½ cups sugar
2 tablespoons cornflour
1 tablespoon ground mustard
1 tablespoon turmeric
1 tablespoon curry powder

1 Drain corn and combine in a non-aluminium pan with onions, capsicums, chillies, garlic, mustard seed and celery seed. Stir in 600 mL of vinegar and bring to the boil.
2 Add sugar and simmer for 20 minutes.

3 Blend cornflour, ground mustard, turmeric, curry powder with remaining vinegar and stir into the hot mixture. Stir until it boils and simmer for 5 minutes before bottling in heated jars.

Sweet Mango Chutney

If you are fortunate enough to have access to unripe mangoes, well and good. But if the only mangoes you get are ripe and ready for eating you can still enjoy this chutney, but do not cook them too long or they will become a purée instead of staying in pieces.

PREPARATION TIME: *30 minutes*
COOKING TIME: *about 1 hour*
MAKES *about 4 cups*

3 or 4 large unripe mangoes
3 teaspoons salt
8 large dried chillies
2 cups white vinegar
5 cloves garlic
½ cup peeled, finely chopped ginger
1 teaspoon garam masala
2 cups sugar
1 cup sultanas or seedless raisins

1 Peel the mangoes and slice thickly, discarding seeds. Put the mango slices in a large glass bowl and sprinkle with the salt.
2 Remove stalks and seeds from chillies, soak them in a little vinegar for 10 minutes and purée in electric blender together with the garlic and ginger. It does not matter if there are still pieces of chilli. (If no blender is available simply break the chillies into small pieces, crush the garlic and finely grate the ginger.)
3 Put remaining vinegar into a stainless steel or other non-aluminium saucepan with the blended mixture, garam masala and sugar. Bring to the boil and simmer, uncovered, for 15 minutes. Add mangoes and sultanas and simmer until thick and syrupy. Cool and put into sterile bottles. Seal airtight.
Note: Green apples, apricots or other suitable fruit may be used in place of mangoes.

Corn Relish

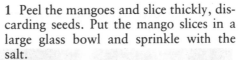

For jams and chutneys, use fruit in good condition. Don't waste valuable time and ingredients on any fruit that is over-ripe or bruised.

Pineapple Chutney

Half-ripe fruit is even better than fully ripe when it comes to jams and chutneys.

PREPARATION TIME: *30 minutes*
COOKING TIME: *about 45 minutes*
MAKES *3 medium jars*

1 large firm pineapple
1 tablespoon salt
2 cups vinegar
1 cup sugar
10 whole cloves
1 stick cinnamon
250 g sultanas
1 tablespoon crushed garlic
2 tablespoons finely chopped fresh ginger
3 fresh or dried chillies, sliced

1 Peel and core the pineapple and weigh it. There should be 700–800 g of prepared fruit. Chop the pineapple, sprinkle with salt and set aside for 2 hours. Drain liquid from pineapple.
2 In a pan, simmer the vinegar, sugar and whole spices for 10 minutes, then add pineapple, sultanas, garlic, ginger and chillies.
3 Continue cooking, stirring occasionally, until thick. Put into clean, hot bottles and cover when cold. Keep for 2 weeks before using.

Fresh Lemon Chutney

PREPARATION TIME: *15 minutes plus overnight soaking*
COOKING TIME: *1½ hours*
MAKES *about 3 cups*

350 g lemons
6 cups water
4 red chillies or 2 teaspoons chilli powder
2 cups white sugar
1 tablespoon crushed garlic
1 tablespoon finely grated ginger
½ cup sultanas
2 teaspoons salt
2 tablespoons ground seed mustard, optional

1 Cut lemons into slices. Put into a non-metal bowl and add 6 cups cold water. Leave to soak overnight.
2 Next day, boil lemons until tender.
3 Add the chillies, sugar, garlic, ginger, sultanas, salt and mustard.
4 Boil uncovered for 30–40 minutes, stirring occasionally at first, and frequently as mixture thickens. Bottle in clean, hot jars and cover when cold, protecting metal lids with a double thickness of greaseproof paper or plastic.

Fresh Lemon Chutney

Harissa

This is the traditional method for making Harissa, a fiery sauce served with Moroccan Couscous. If you have a liking for spicy food a jar of this in your refrigerator will let you add instant zest to just about anything you cook. But do use it sparingly — a little is good, a lot is not necessarily better!

PREPARATION TIME: *15 minutes plus soaking time for traditional method*
COOKING TIME: *nil*
MAKES *1 small jar*

50 g fresh hot red chillies or 20 g dried chillies
3–4 cloves garlic, peeled
1 teaspoon ground coriander
1 teaspoon ground cumin
1 teaspoon dried mint leaves
1 teaspoon salt
2 tablespoons chopped fresh coriander

1 With kitchen scissors, snip off stems and remove seeds from chillies. (For an even hotter sauce, leave the seeds in.) If using dried chillies, rinse them, then put them in a bowl. Pour boiling water over and leave them to soak for an hour or longer. Drain, reserving the water.
2 Put prepared chillies with all the other ingredients into a blender and purée to a paste, using a little of the soaking water to facilitate blending; or, more authentically, pound to a paste with mortar and pestle. (For a quick version of Harissa, combine 4 tablespoons of bottled crushed fresh chillies, or sambal oelek, with 2 teaspoons crushed garlic and the rest of the ingredients and blend well.)
3 Turn into a small glass jar, cover the top with a thin layer of olive oil and store in the refrigerator. Use sparingly, replacing oil to cover the surface each time.

Smoky, Spicy Barbecue Sauce

This sauce keeps well in a bottle and can be used to brush over pork spare ribs, chicken joints, lobsters or prawns while cooking, either on a barbecue, under a grill or in the oven. The flavour is incredibly delicious.

PREPARATION TIME: *5 minutes*
COOKING TIME: *10 minutes*
MAKES *sufficient for 1.5 kg main ingredient*

½ cup bottled tomato sauce
¼ cup chilli sauce
¼ cup brown sugar
1 tablespoon vinegar
3–4 cloves garlic crushed with 1 teaspoon salt
½ teaspoon black pepper
1 teaspoon garlic salt or 1 teaspoon hickory smoked salt

Combine all the ingredients in a small non-aluminium saucepan and stir over low heat until sugar dissolves. Simmer for 10 minutes, stirring now and then. Cool and store in a jar in the refrigerator.

Rouille

This could be described as a chilli and garlic mayonnaise which is traditionally served with Provençal fish soup and bouillabaisse but is also nice served with cooked or raw vegetables as a dip and in any context where a rich, smooth, pungent sauce is required. I use the blender mayonnaise method because it is so quick and easy.

PREPARATION TIME: *5 minutes*
COOKING TIME: *nil*
MAKES *1 cup*

5 cloves garlic, peeled
¾ teaspoon salt
1 egg yolk
¾ cup extra virgin olive oil
¼ cup chopped canned pimiento or 1 teaspoon paprika
1 fresh red chilli or hot chilli sauce to taste

1 Put the garlic, salt, egg yolk, pimiento and seeded chilli into the container of an electric blender and blend on high speed for 10 seconds.
2 Through the hole in cap of blender jar add the olive oil a little at a time. As mixture thickens, the oil may be added in a thin stream. This sauce will keep for a week in the refrigerator stored in a screw top jar, but should be served at room temperature.

Smoky, Spicy Barbecue Sauce glazing American-style pork ribs

Paprika, a mild and sweet powder made from capsicums, is the essential flavouring of many Hungarian dishes including chicken paprikas and goulash. The best paprika comes from Hungary and tales are told that in the past, poorer paprika would be adulterated with red lead to give it the right colour!

Subtle Marinade

Ideal with beef, good with pork, probably too subtle for lamb. Try this on a 10 cm thick slice of rump and barbecue on a rotisserie or roast in the oven, basting frequently.

PREPARATION TIME: *10 minutes*
COOKING TIME: *nil*
MAKES *sufficient for 1.5 kg beef in one piece which will serve 8–10, or 1 kg American style spare ribs, which will serve 4–6*

1 teaspoon juniper berries
1 tablespoon whole black peppercorns
1 teaspoon ground allspice
2 teaspoons Worcestershire sauce
2 or 3 cloves of garlic
1 teaspoon salt
1 tablespoon chopped chives
1 teaspoon dried oregano
¼ cup vermouth
¼ cup extra virgin olive oil

1 Crush the juniper berries and black peppercorns coarsely. On a wooden board, use the flat of a knife to crush the garlic to a paste with the salt. Combine these with all the other ingredients.
2 Pour over the meat to be marinated and set aside for at least two hours, turning it every half hour.
3 Barbecue over coals which have reached the stage where they are covered with a fine white ash. If using a covered barbecue the meat should be done medium rare in about 45 minutes. In a moderate oven, allow 50 minutes per kilo. For spareribs allow about 1 hour. During cooking, brush with the marinade every 15 minutes.

Peanut Sauce

I am always trying out new recipes but this is an old favourite that I have made dozens of times. The reason? It is the best peanut sauce I have ever tasted. The sauce base will keep for weeks or months in a glass jar in the refrigerator. When coconut milk is added to thin it down it must be used within a day or two. But it is not just a sauce for vegetables or satays . . . try it as a spread on toast or biscuits to serve as canapés.

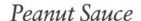

PREPARATION TIME: *25 minutes*
COOKING TIME: *5 minutes*
MAKES *2 cups base which, mixed with water or coconut milk, will yield about 5 cups sauce*

½ cup peanut oil
1–2 teaspoons dried garlic flakes or instant minced garlic
3 tablespoons dried onion flakes
2 or 3 large dried chillies
1 teaspoon dried shrimp paste
1 tablespoon lemon juice
1 tablespoon soy sauce
1 × 375 g jar crunchy peanut butter
1½ tablespoons coarse raw sugar

1 Heat the oil in a wok until only medium hot or the dried garlic and onion will burn. Immerse garlic flakes on a wire strainer for a few seconds and lift them out before they turn brown. Drain on absorbent paper. Fry onion flakes in the same way, again taking care not to leave them in the oil too long. Drain and cool.
2 Fry the whole chillies until they are puffed and crisp, and have turned black, about 1 minute. Drain and cool, then discard the stalks and seeds and crumble or chop the chillies into small pieces. Set aside with the garlic and onions.
3 Add the shrimp paste to the oil remaining in the wok, crushing it with the back of a spoon. Pour into a bowl and stir in lemon juice and soy sauce, add peanut butter and stir until well blended. Leave until quite cold.
4 Add the crisp garlic and onion flakes, crumbled chillies and sugar. Mix and put into a screw top jar to store. Use this thick mixture as a spread. For a sauce, take some from the jar and mix with water or diluted coconut milk until it is of a pouring consistency. Taste and adjust with more salt, sugar or lemon juice as necessary.

Salsa Cruda

This uncooked tomato sauce is very popular in Mexican cuisine, the addition of fresh chillies giving it a definite buzz.

PREPARATION TIME: *15 minutes*
COOKING TIME: *nil*
SERVES *4–6*

4 firm ripe tomatoes
2 fresh hot chillies
1 white or purple onion
¼ cup chopped fresh coriander
1 teaspoon salt
¼ teaspoon pepper
1 teaspoon sugar

1 Scald the tomatoes or hold them over a gas flame until the skin splits, then plunge them into iced water until cold. Peel the tomatoes, cut in halves crossways and gently squeeze out and discard the seeds. Dice the tomato flesh finely.
2 Seed and chop the chillies. Chop the onion very finely. Combine all the ingredients, cover and chill.

Green Salsa

A tart accompaniment to many dishes. Tomatillos are used in Mexico, but firm green tomatoes are a good substitute.

PREPARATION TIME: *10 minutes plus 30 minutes standing time*
COOKING TIME: *nil*
SERVES 6–8

4 green tomatoes
1 small red onion, finely chopped
2 fresh green chillies, seeded and chopped
½ cup chopped fresh coriander
1 tablespoon olive oil
2 teaspoons white wine vinegar
½ teaspoon salt

1 Wash the tomatoes and with a stainless

knife cut into very fine dice. Combine with the rest of the ingredients.
2 Put into a non-metal bowl, cover and set aside for 30 minutes before serving to allow flavours to develop.

Mint Chutney

Another fresh, uncooked chutney which may be used as an accompaniment to rice and curries, or as a dip for savoury snacks.

PREPARATION TIME: *10 minutes*
COOKING TIME: *nil*
MAKES *about 1¼ cups*

1 cup firmly packed mint leaves
3 or 4 spring onions, including green leaves
2 fresh green chillies, seeded and sliced
½ teaspoon chopped garlic
1 teaspoon salt
2 teaspoons sugar
1 teaspoon garam masala
½ cup lime or lemon juice

Put the mint leaves, chopped spring onions and all the other ingredients into an electric blender (a food processor will not give the correct consistency) and purée until smooth. Add a little water if necessary to facilitate blending. Pour into a bowl, cover and chill. This chutney has a beautiful green colour on the first day it is made but although the colour will darken on being kept, it is perfectly good to eat even 3 or 4 days later.

Peanut Sauce served over steamed vegetables

Green Salsa and Salsa Cruda

SPICE BLENDS & FLAVOUR ACCENTS

I prefer using individual spices rather than commercial blends. In this way, the cook has the freedom to emphasise favourite flavours, and play down others.

Even when of the highest quality, commercial curry powders, garam masala and so on are made to a formula which remains inflexible. The magic of spicing is the ability to change combinations and proportions, thereby creating dishes with their own individual flavours.

However, there are certain spice combinations which are very useful to have on hand — provided, of course, that one does not use them in every dish. To save the trouble of combining half a dozen spices in the tiny quantities needed for a single dish, I prepare sufficient for a number of dishes and store the mixture in an airtight container in the freezer. This way the fragrance and flavour are preserved much better than when exposed to light and heat. Save empty spice and herb jars for your own spice mixes.

Here are some blends which will come in useful for many of the recipes in this book of spicy food.

Panch Phora

'Panch' means five in Hindi, and panch phora is a combination of five different aromatic seeds which are used whole, not ground.

> 2 tablespoons black mustard seeds
> 2 tablespoons cumin seeds
> 2 tablespoons nigella (kalonji)
> 1 tablespoon fenugreek seeds
> 1 tablespoon fennel seeds

Combine in a glass jar with well fitting lid. Shake before use to ensure even distribution.

Creole Frying Mix

A skilful blending of herbs and spices with ground rice which gives a nice, crisp coating to fish or chicken which is shallow-fried.

> 2 tablespoons ground rice
> 2 tablespoons plain flour
> 2 tablespoons ground black pepper
> 1 tablespoon salt
> 1 tablespoon garlic powder
> 1 tablespoon paprika
> 2 teaspoons ground oregano
> 2 teaspoons chilli powder

Combine all the ingredients in a glass jar and shake well before using.

Creole Seasoning

Useful to have ready mixed in a bottle, then giving that enticing Creole flavour to various dishes is only a sprinkle away. For instance, try seasoning a batch of freshly popped corn with the merest touch of this mixture . . . it's addictive!

> 2 tablespoons paprika
> 1½ tablespoons table salt
> 1 tablespoon onion powder
> 1 tablespoon garlic powder
> 2 teaspoons ground black pepper
> 1 teaspoon cayenne pepper
> 1 teaspoon ground dried thyme
> 1 teaspoon ground dried oregano

Combine all the ingredients thoroughly and store in an air-tight container.

Garam Masala

I prefer to make this aromatic spice blend from whole spices, first roasting them lightly until fragrant, then grinding them in an electric blender to a fine powder. It is worth the time and trouble taken.

Traditional Method

4 tablespoons coriander seeds
2 tablespoons cumin seeds
1 tablespoon whole black peppercorns
2 teaspoons cardamom seeds (measure after roasting and removing pods)
4 × 7 cm cinnamon sticks
1 teaspoon whole cloves
1 whole nutmeg

1 In a small dry pan, roast separately the coriander, cumin, peppercorns, cardamom pods, cinnamon and cloves. As each one starts to smell fragrant, turn onto a plate and leave to cool. The roasting brings out the flavours and makes the spices brittle and easier to grind to powder.
2 Peel the cardamoms, discard pods and use only the seeds. Put all the spices into an electric blender and blend to a fine powder. Finely grate the nutmeg and mix in. Store in a glass jar with tight-fitting lid and keep it out of heat and light. Always use a dry spoon and replace lid securely.

Quick Method

If the above method seems like too much work, combine the same spices purchased in ground form. But again, roast them lightly in a dry pan, shaking or stirring over medium heat and taking care they don't burn. There should be only enough heat to bring out their fragrance.

2 tablespoons ground coriander
1 tablespoon ground cumin
2 teaspoons ground black pepper
3 teaspoons ground cardamom
1½ tablespoons ground cinnamon
1 teaspoon ground cloves
2 teaspoons ground nutmeg

1 In a small pan, roast the ground coriander, cumin and pepper over low heat, shaking the pan or stirring constantly. As soon as they smell fragrant, turn onto a plate.
2 Combine the fragrant spices — cardamom, cinnamon, cloves and nutmeg and roast very lightly for only a minute or two, then mix with the first spices. Allow to cool completely before putting into a bottle.

1 *Roast coriander seeds in a small dry pan until fragrant.*

2 *Turn coriander on to a plate to cool, roast remaining spices separately until fragrant.*

3 *Peel cardamoms, discard pod and use only the seeds.*

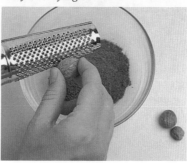

4 *Finely grate a whole nutmeg over blended spices.*

SUGAR & SPICE (SWEET SPICES)

It is surprising how many people assume that spicy food is also hot, pungent food. Just stop and think of foods such as plum pudding and mince pies. Aromatic spices are what give them their special fragrance but there's nothing in the least 'hot' about them — unless, of course, they are fresh out of the oven or the steamer. Even if you do not like hot flavours, here are some ideas for adding extra dash to your food.

Cinnamon sugar Combine one part ground cinnamon with 4 parts caster sugar. Store in a tightly stoppered jar and sprinkle on French toast, waffles, pancakes, muffins.

Combine one tablespoon cinnamon with 4 tablespoons caster sugar to make cinnamon sugar.

Add a vanilla bean to a 250 g jar of caster sugar, store for one week to make vanilla sugar.

Vanilla sugar Store vanilla beans in a jar of caster sugar or granulated sugar, *or* grind used, washed and well dried vanilla pods in electric blender with icing sugar. Use to make biscuits or to sift over biscuits or cakes after baking.

Spiced syrup Infuse 2 sticks cinnamon, 20 whole cloves and 1 vanilla bean in sugar syrup made by simmering 2 cups sugar and 2 cups water with the spices for 20 minutes. Cover and leave until cold. Bottle and strain over fruit salad, chill and serve.

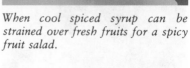

Add cinnamon sticks, cloves and a vanilla bean to simmering sugar syrup, stand for 20 minutes.

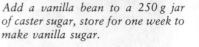

When cool spiced syrup can be strained over fresh fruits for a spicy fruit salad.

Cardamom sugar Store cardamom pods in a bottle of sugar and use to sweeten coffee for an exotic flavour. Add to apples when stewing, for an unusual touch of spice.

Clove sugar Mix ground cloves with caster sugar in the proportion 1 part in 20 as it is a strong-flavoured spice and a little goes a long way. Use as cinnamon sugar.

Nutmeg sugar Grate one nutmeg on the finest grater, mix with ½ cup caster sugar and keep for sprinkling over custards or bread puddings, apple tarts or cheesecakes before baking.

Star anise Infuse custard with star anise and freeze for ice cream or pour over hot puddings or fruit.

Ginger One spice which finds itself equally at home among hot spices or sweets, ginger can be quite pungent when mature, but such is the popularity of its flavour that it is used to enliven savoury sauces as well as cakes, biscuits and frozen desserts.

SOME LIKE IT HOT (HOT SPICES)

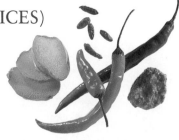

There are some spices which should come with a printed warning! If you are not familiar with the territory, tread warily when you taste certain of the flavours which are indispensable but should be used in tiny amounts. Here they are, with some notes on how to enjoy them.

Ginger

There is a dipping sauce used in Chinese cuisine to add spice to delicate meats such as steamed chicken. It is delicious. Finely grate fresh ginger and mix it with peanut oil which has been used to fry onions and garlic, then allowed to cool. The proportions are 2 tablespoons grated ginger to 1 tablespoon oil. A little hot chilli may be mixed in. Even a plain roast chicken becomes inspiring when treated to this dip. Use sparingly to enhance, not to overpower.

Chillies

Of course everyone knows chillies can be mild, hot or very hot. But many have no idea what constitutes a safe amount. Assuming we are dealing with hot chillies, a slice taken with a mouthful of other food is plenty to add excitement. If chillies are ground into a sauce, a couple of drops on a bite-sized piece of food is enough. Note that chillies are always to be taken as an accent on other food, never on their own. When adding chillies, fresh or dried, to cooked food, follow guidelines given in individual recipes.

As you build up a tolerance and start to enjoy hot flavours you may decide to be more adventurous. But for beginners, remember that discretion is to be observed. Don't show off — the results can be painful . . . your tongue will seemingly be on fire and you will get the feeling smoke is coming out of your ears too! If you have been foolhardy enough to chew and swallow a sizable piece of chilli, eat spoon-fuls of plain yoghurt, or plain rice, or drink cold milk. Don't try to cool the burning with fizzy drinks such as lemonade or sparkling wine. Each tiny bubble bursting on your tongue will feel like fireworks going off.

Wasabi

The same advice applies to wasabi — Japanese green horseradish which is an indispensable part of sushi and sashimi. Approach with caution and you will find it quite enjoyable. It offers a totally different kind of 'heat' to chilli. Take too much and it penetrates your nasal passages, burns out your sinuses and scorches your brain like a flame-thrower . . . or that's what it feels like, anyway.

The pale green powder is meant to be mixed with water to make a paste, and only a touch of this paste is then mixed with shoyu to make a dipping sauce for sashimi, or spread very sparingly on sushi.

Mustard

Hot English mustard is an anomaly. Among all the blandness of standard English food lurks this landmine which can take you unawares. I remember a sandwich which had been spread too generously . . . It made a lasting impression, and pity the little girl who grabbed some mustard and popped it in her mouth before her parents could stop her. Keep such condiments out of the reach of small fry.

Mustard should be mixed with cold water at least ten minutes before use for it to develop full flavour.

Green herb mustard can sometimes be found in jars in good delicatessens but it is easy to make. It will keep well in an airtight jar in the refrigerator. A selection of blanched fresh herbs is added to German or French style mustard. You will need about 2 tablespoons each of finely chopped parsley and chives and 2 teaspoons each of basil, thyme and tarragon. Dip them in boiling water for 10–15 seconds, scoop out on a fine strainer and plunge into iced water to set the colour. Drain well. Put into a blender jar with enough mild vinegar to facilitate blending. When they are puréed, add half a cup of Dijon or other smooth mild mustard and blend again.

Desserts & Teatime Treats

HERE IS WHERE SWEET SPICES come into their own! Who can think of Christmas and not associate it with sweet things to eat, most of them fragrant with spice. The scent of cloves and cinnamon, cardamom, ginger and allspice, evoke memories as few other smells can. As well as the rich and traditional, I've included some simple recipes. Health-conscious but no less delicious, they rely on a whiff of exotica to give them that extra special appeal. Some of these desserts are old favourites with a new twist. Others are new — Honey Spice Mousse and an ice-cream redolent with spices... I created them for this book. Whether old or new, I hope you enjoy them as much as we do.

Steamed Ginger Pudding (page 95) and Clove, Cinnamon and Honey Ice-cream (page 98), served with golden syrup and cream 93

Date Pie with Cognac Cream

Spice-flavoured Bavarian cream fills the nut crust of this dessert pie.

PREPARATION TIME: *45 minutes*
COOKING TIME: *10 minutes*
MAKES *one 23 cm pie*

1 cup crushed wheatmeal biscuits
½ cup finely chopped Brazil nuts or blanched almonds
2 tablespoons caster sugar
5 tablespoons melted butter

FILLING
200 g fresh dates or dessert dates
1 tablespoon gelatine
⅓ cup cold water
3 egg yolks
½ cup caster sugar
1 cup milk
½ teaspoon freshly grated nutmeg
½ teaspoon ground cinnamon
⅛ teaspoon ground cloves
1 egg white
300 mL thickened cream
3 teaspoons cognac

1 Combine biscuit crumbs, nuts, sugar and butter until evenly mixed. Press against base and sides of a 23 cm pie plate to form a thin, even layer. Bake in a moderately hot oven (190°C), for 8–10 minutes. Remove from oven and leave to cool.
2 To make the filling, put the dates in a small bowl and pour boiling water over to cover. Set aside for 15–20 minutes, then slit and remove the thin outer skin and the seeds. Cut the dates into thin strips, crossways.
3 Sprinkle gelatine over cold water, leave 5 minutes to soften, and dissolve in a microwave oven or over simmering water.
4 Whisk egg yolks with half the sugar until thick and light. Bring the milk to the boil and add gradually to eggs, stirring. Return to the saucepan and stir briskly and constantly over very low heat until custard thickens and coats the back of a metal spoon. Remove from heat, stir in the gelatine, dates and spices and cool until as thick as unbeaten egg whites.
5 In a clean, dry bowl, whisk the egg white until stiff but not dry. Add all but a tablespoon of the sugar and whisk again until smooth and glossy.
6 Whip the cream with the remaining sugar and the cognac until holding soft peaks. Fold the egg white and half the whipped cream into the custard and pour into the cooled pastry shell. Chill until set. Pipe the remaining whipped cream and decorate the top of the pie as desired.

Low-fat Christmas Pudding

We all know how rich a Christmas pudding can be, but here's a low-fat version that has no suet, no butter, not even one egg yolk. Hardly traditional, but wonderful for health-conscious revellers. The reason it tastes good is that all the spiciness is still there. Leftover pudding heats marvellously in the microwave oven.

PREPARATION TIME: *30 minutes*
COOKING TIME: *2 hours*
SERVES *6–8*

2 cups mixed dried fruit such as sultanas, currants, chopped raisins, dates and prunes
¼ cup chopped almonds (optional)
½ cup brown sugar
1 cup fresh breadcrumbs
1 apple, peeled and coarsely grated
1 cup plain flour
1 teaspoon bicarbonate of soda
½ teaspoon ground nutmeg
½ teaspoon ground cinnamon
½ teaspoon ground cardamom
¼ teaspoon ground cloves
1 teaspoon finely grated lemon rind
¼ cup corn or sunflower oil
3 egg whites, lightly beaten
¾ cup warm, low-fat milk

1 Put the fruit, almonds, sugar and breadcrumbs into a large bowl and toss together. Sift the flour with the bicarbonate of soda and spices, sprinkle over the fruit mixture and toss again.
2 Stir together the lemon rind, oil, egg whites and milk. Pour over the other ingredients and mix well. Line an oiled, heatproof pudding bowl with a circle of non-stick baking paper, making slits in the paper so that it will overlap and fit

Low-fat Christmas Pudding served with custard

Cardamom can be richly fragrant, or weak and lacking in flavour because it has been mixed with other, less expensive spices. Even honest-to-goodness cardamom can be the whole pods ground up, or only the seeds. The latter is much stronger. It is also, necessarily, more expensive.

snugly in the bowl. This will prevent the pudding sticking to the bowl.

3 Turn the mixture into the bowl and, if you are not using a pudding bowl with a snap-on lid, tie a double thickness of wide, heavy duty foil like a lid over the top. Make a handle with the string so that it is easy to lift the pudding out of the steamer. Place the bowl on a trivet and pour boiling water into the saucepan to come half-way up the side of the bowl. Cover and boil for 2 hours, replenishing the water with more boiling water as it boils away. Serve with custard.

Steamed Ginger Puddings

Steamed puddings put me in mind of cold winter evenings and hearty family dinners but these small, ginger-rich steamed puddings are delicate enough to grace your dinner party menu.

PREPARATION TIME: *20 minutes*
COOKING TIME: *35 minutes*
SERVES 6–8

1½ cups plain flour
½ teaspoon bicarbonate of soda
3 teaspoons ground ginger
100 g butter
½ cup brown sugar
2 eggs
¼ cup golden syrup
½ cup milk
½ cup chopped glacé ginger
melted butter for moulds
1 cup cream, whipped
extra glacé ginger for decorating

1 Sift flour, bicarbonate of soda and ground ginger together. Cream butter and brown sugar until light, add 1 egg and beat well, then mix in half the dry ingredients.
2 Add the remaining egg, beat well and mix in the remaining flour. Stir in the golden syrup and add the milk gradually. Fold in the chopped ginger.
3 Brush individual ½ cup moulds with melted butter and spoon in the pudding batter until they are two-thirds full — they will rise quite a lot. Cover each one with a circle of buttered greaseproof paper.

4 Place on a rack in a steamer and steam over fast boiling water for 45 minutes, replenishing the water as it boils away. Remove lid and allow steam to escape for a few minutes.
5 Peel off the paper and turn out puddings. Serve with whipped cream or ice-cream and extra glacé ginger or drizzle with a little golden syrup.

Honey Spice Mousse

Cloves, nutmeg and honey give a delicate yet exotic flavour to this light dessert. It is economical, too — the modest outlay of ingredients fills 8 mousse pots.

PREPARATION TIME: *15 minutes plus 3 hours freezing time*
COOKING TIME: *7 minutes*
SERVES 8

2 eggs
2 tablespoons honey
2 tablespoons sugar
½ cup water
15 whole cloves
1 cup cream
½ teaspoon freshly grated nutmeg

1 Put yolks of eggs in one bowl and whites in another.
2 In a small, heavy saucepan put the honey, sugar, water and the whole cloves. Stir over medium heat until sugar dissolves, then boil hard for 5 minutes. While syrup boils, whisk the egg whites to a stiff froth.
3 Remove cloves, and pour half the hot syrup onto the egg whites, beating until thick, glossy and cool. Bring remaining syrup to boiling point once more and pour onto the egg yolks, whisking until light. Cool to room temperature.
4 Whip the cream until thick but not stiff. Gently stir egg yolks and cream together, adding the freshly grated nutmeg. Fold in the egg whites. Spoon into 8 small mousse pots and place in the freezer until required, or for at least 3 hours. Serve with a crisp sweet biscuit, or fresh berries.

To store your vanilla pods, bury them in a jar of icing sugar or caster sugar. When they have been infused they may be washed, dried very well, and used again.
In a school of pâtisserie I attended in France, used vanilla pods were dried, then ground with icing sugar and the resulting mixture used in cakes and biscuits. To make pure vanilla essence, cut a pod into small pieces and soak in brandy or vodka for at least 3 months.

Spiced Apple Pie

Spiced Apple Pie

Apple pie with its tart filling is always a favourite, never more so than when its rich, sweet pastry has an extra flavour.

PREPARATION TIME: *30 minutes plus 30 minutes chilling time*
COOKING TIME: *35–40 minutes*
SERVES *6–8*

PASTRY
2 cups plain flour
¼ teaspoon salt
¼ teaspoon ground cloves
2 tablespoons caster sugar
125 g butter
about 5 tablespoons cold water

FILLING
1 kg cooking apples
½ cup sugar
2 tablespoons plain flour
½ teaspoon ground cardamom
egg white for brushing
1 tablespoon caster sugar

1 Sift flour with salt and cloves; stir in sugar. Rub in butter, then add cold water and mix to a dough. Wrap and chill for about 30 minutes.
2 Roll out slightly more than half of the pastry very thinly and line a 20 cm pie plate, leaving the edges hanging over. Roll out remaining pastry to make a lid and set aside, covered with plastic to prevent drying out.
3 Peel, core and slice apples, toss in sugar, flour and spice and arrange in pastry-lined pie plate.
4 Place pastry lid over the apples and trim edges. Moisten edges and pinch together, fluting or crimping them for a decorative edge.
5 Brush top of pie with lightly beaten egg white and sprinkle lightly with caster sugar. With a sharp knife, make a few slashes in the top to let steam escape. Bake in a hot oven (200°C) for 35–40 minutes or until golden brown.
6 Serve hot with thickened cream or Whisky and Cinnamon Sauce (page 101).

Date and Nut Pie

An especially rich and sweet pie for those who enjoy desserts that make no concessions to calories.

PREPARATION TIME: *20 minutes*
COOKING TIME: *1 hour*
MAKES *one 23 cm pie*

PASTRY
1 small egg
¼ cup caster sugar
90 g soft butter
1¼ cups plain flour
½ teaspoon baking powder

FILLING
1 cup chopped, seeded dates
1 cup cream
1 teaspoon ground nutmeg
1 teaspoon ground cinnamon
½ teaspoon allspice or ¼ teaspoon ground cloves
125 g butter
⅓ cup lightly packed brown sugar
⅓ cup white sugar
4 egg yolks
2 tablespoons plain flour
½ cup walnuts or pecans, roughly chopped

1 Whisk egg and sugar until thick and light. Add the soft butter and beat until smooth, then fold in the sifted dry ingredients to form a dough. In hot weather, wrap and chill for 20 minutes. Roll out between two sheets of plastic, and line a lightly greased 23 cm pie plate.
2 Combine dates and cream and bring almost to boiling point. Remove from heat and stir in spices. Cool to lukewarm, stirring occasionally.
3 Cream butter and both kinds of sugar until light and beat in egg yolks one at a time. Add flour and beat well.
4 Fold in warm date mixture and nuts, pour into prepared pastry shell and bake in a preheated moderate oven (180°C) for 10 minutes, then reduce heat to 160°C and bake 40 minutes or until pie is set. Test with a thin knife blade in centre. Pie will not be firm, only set. Watch carefully and if crust browns too quickly, cover edges with strips of foil.
5 Serve warm or cold with sweetened whipped cream or with one of the spicy ice-creams in this chapter.

Back: Date and Nut Pie, Front: Date Pie with Cognac Cream (page 97)

Clove, Cinnamon and Honey Ice-cream

Infusing whole cloves and cinnamon quills gives a more delicate flavour than using ground spices. It also keeps the colour of the ice cream pale and pretty. If using an electric churn with its own freezing unit, the ice-cream is ready in about 20 minutes. Still freezing takes longer.

PREPARATION TIME: *20 minutes plus 1 hour standing time and freezing time*
COOKING TIME: *15 minutes*
SERVES 6–8

2 cups milk
20 whole cloves
2 × 7 cm sticks cinnamon
3 egg yolks
1 whole egg
¼ cup sugar
¼ cup honey
150 mL cream

1 In an enamel or other non-aluminium saucepan, heat the milk with the whole cloves and cinnamon quills, stirring, until milk reaches simmering point. Turn off heat, cover pan and leave to infuse for 1 hour. Better still, refrigerate overnight so that the flavour of the spices will permeate the milk with greater effect.
2 Put the egg yolks and whole egg into a bowl and whisk with the sugar until light. Return the milk and spices to the boil, stirring. Pour a ladleful of the hot milk into the egg mixture and mix, then add yolk mixture to the pan and cook over very low heat, stirring briskly all the time, until the custard thickens. If you are watchful you can do this over direct heat and it only takes a few minutes, but do not let it approach simmering point or it will curdle.
3 Remove from the heat at once and stand the pan in a bowl of iced water to cool it quickly. Stir in the honey until dissolved. Strain the custard into another bowl and discard the spices. Cover and chill the custard until very cold.
4 If freezing in a gelato machine, stir the unwhipped cream into the custard. Freeze in the machine, which will take 15–20 minutes according to the type used. Serve the ice cream straight away or transfer it to a bowl and cover the surface with a

sheet of freezer plastic. Store in the freezer until shortly before required, then leave at room temperature for a few minutes to allow ice cream to soften slightly. **Note:** If not using a churn, turn the freezer to its coldest setting when starting to make the custard. Whip the cream until thick but not stiff and stir into the chilled custard. Pour into a shallow container and freeze until firm, then return setting to normal.

Star Anise Ice-cream

An unusual flavour in ice-cream, but those who like its licorice taste really go for it. Use pieces of star anise (there is usually a high proportion of broken 'stars' in a packet) to measure a tablespoonful.

PREPARATION TIME: *10 minutes*
COOKING TIME: *20 minutes.*
SERVES 8

3 cups milk
1 tablespoon star anise
½ vanilla bean (optional)
1 cup sugar
4 egg yolks
300 mL cream

1 Put the milk, star anise, vanilla bean and ½ cup sugar into a non-aluminium saucepan and stir over gentle heat until milk is almost at boiling point.
2 In a bowl, beat the egg yolks with remaining sugar until thick and light. Ladle some of the hot milk into the yolks, stirring briskly, then pour back into the saucepan and cook, stirring constantly, over lowest heat until the custard thickens sufficiently to coat the back of a metal spoon. Remove from heat, stir in the cream and stand the pan in cold water to cool the custard quickly. Cover and refrigerate overnight so it will be strongly infused with the flavour of star anise.
3 Strain the custard and freeze in an electric churn or in freezer trays. If not churned, the ice-cream will be smoother if stirred two or three times when half frozen. Let the ice-cream soften slightly before serving with a crisp biscuit.

Vanilla could not be commercially grown outside Mexico until a way was discovered to hand-pollinate the flowers. Certain species of bee and humming bird, only present in Mexico and Central America, were responsible for the pollination of the flower which only stayed open for 24 hours. The method invented in 1841 by a former French slave is still in commercial use.

Shrikhand

Shrikhand is thick yoghurt, sweetened and flavoured with saffron, cardamom and rosewater, then chilled. Sprinkle with chopped unsalted pistachios before serving. Shrikhand originates in northern India, where it is known as the Honeymoon Sweet. I don't know why.

PREPARATION TIME: *15 minutes*
COOKING TIME: *nil*
SERVES *4–6*

400 g country-style (thick) yoghurt
3–4 tablespoons caster sugar
2 drops rose flavouring
⅛ teaspoon ground cardamom seeds
¼ teaspoon saffron strands (loosely packed)
1 tablespoon pistachio kernels

1 Put the yoghurt into a bowl with the sugar, flavouring and ground cardamom and mix together. Lightly toast the saffron strands in a small pan over low heat, watching carefully for signs of darkening because they must not burn. Turn out onto a plate to cool. Crush with back of spoon and dissolve in a tablespoon of boiling water.
2 Stir into the yoghurt, turn into a serving bowl or individual mousse pots, cover and chill.
3 Blanch the pistachio kernels in boiling water for 30 seconds, drain and cool, then chop finely. Sprinkle over the surface of Shrikhand before serving.

Shrikhand

1 *Lightly toast the saffron strands in a small pan over low heat.*

2 *Turn onto a plate to cool, crush saffron with a spoon and dissolve in a little water.*

3 *Stir dissolved saffron into yoghurt mixture, pour into serving dish, cover and chill.*

Cloves and cardamom are used as breath-sweeteners in the East. Young Indian men visiting the objects of their affection often chew on cardamom seeds to perfume their breath. Tradition has it that in the third century BC Chinese courtiers were ordered to carry cloves in their mouths when addressing the emperor.

Ginger Parfait

This recipe requires some concentration to have the egg whites whisked and ready for the syrup the minute it is removed from the heat.

PREPARATION TIME: *10 minutes*
COOKING TIME: *about 8 minutes*
SERVES 8

½ cup sugar
½ cup water
1 teaspoon gelatine
1 tablespoon cold water
2 egg whites
⅓ cup finely chopped glacé ginger
300 mL cream

1 Put sugar and water into a heavy saucepan and set over moderate heat. Sprinkle the gelatine over the cold water in a cup and leave to soften while syrup comes to the boil. Stir until sugar dissolves, then boil the syrup hard for 5 minutes without stirring. It should be thick enough to spin a thread. Remove from heat and stir softened gelatine into the syrup.
2 While syrup cooks, whisk the egg whites until stiff but not dry. Pour the hot syrup slowly onto them, whisking until thick, glossy and completely cool.
3 Fold in the ginger, and then the cream which has been whipped until thick but not stiff. Pour into freezer tray, cover with foil and freeze until firm.

Cardamom Fudge

Cardamom Fudge

A small sweet something to serve with coffee after dinner.

PREPARATION TIME: *5 minutes*
COOKING TIME: *about 30 minutes*
MAKES *about 25 squares*

¾ cup milk
410 g can sweetened condensed milk
1½ cups sugar
60 g butter
2 teaspoons vanilla essence
1 teaspoon ground cardamom

1 Butter a square 20 cm pan or dish.
2 In a heavy saucepan combine milk, condensed milk, sugar and butter and stir over medium heat until boiling.
3 Boil, stirring, until it reaches the soft ball stage which is 114°C on a sugar thermometer. To test mixture without a thermometer, first remove pan from heat so mixture will not overcook then drop a little of the mixture into a glass of iced water to see if it forms a soft ball.
4 Let mixture cool slightly, then add vanilla essence and cardamom. Beat until fudge thickens and just starts to lose its gloss. Quickly pour into buttered dish.
5 When firm, cut into squares with a sharp knife.

Rich Bread Pudding

A luxury version of a homely favourite.

PREPARATION TIME: *about 1 hour*
COOKING TIME: *about 35 minutes*
SERVES 8

3 eggs
2 cups milk
¾ cup sugar
3 teaspoons vanilla
300 g day-old bread, diced
½ cup glacé ginger
¼ cup glacé cherries
½ cup blanched almonds or raw cashew nuts
¼ cup sultanas
30 g soft butter
30 g cold butter

1 Beat the eggs, add the milk and all but 2 tablespoons of the sugar and stir to dissolve. Stir in vanilla. Drop in the bread, crusts and all, and set aside to soak for 20 minutes.
2 Slice ginger and cherries, and chop the nuts. Set aside half the nuts with the reserved sugar for sprinkling over the top.
3 Generously grease a large square or rectangular ovenproof dish with the soft butter and preheat oven to moderate (180°C).
4 Add fruit and remaining nuts to the bread and egg mixture and mix well. Pour into prepared dish and scatter reserved sugar and nuts over the top. Dot with cold butter cut into tiny pieces.
5 Bake for 35 minutes or until puffed and golden on top. Allow to cool slightly, then cut in large squares and serve with Whisky and Cinnamon Sauce (page 101).

Cardamom is the third most costly spice in the world, coming after saffron and vanilla.

Whisky and Cinnamon Sauce

Use a heavy-based non-aluminium saucepan for making this sauce as aluminium will discolour the custard.

PREPARATION TIME: *15 minutes*
COOKING TIME: *15 minutes*
MAKES *1½ cups*

3 egg yolks
¼ cup sugar
1 cup milk
1 stick cinnamon
¼ cup whisky

1 Whisk the eggs with half the sugar until thick and light.
2 Put remaining sugar into a heavy non-aluminium saucepan with milk and cinnamon stick and place over a low heat. Stir the milk until it just reaches simmering point.
3 Ladle hot milk onto the whisked yolks, stirring constantly, then return mixture to pan and cook over very low heat, stirring, until the custard thickens enough to coat the back of a spoon. It must not boil or even reach a simmer, or it will curdle.
4 As soon as the custard thickens, pour into a serving dish and leave to cool to room temperature. Remove cinnamon stick, stir in whisky and serve.

Figs with Ginger

An economical and easy-to-make dessert.

PREPARATION TIME: *5 minutes*
COOKING TIME: *15 minutes*
SERVES 6

18 dried figs
12 thin slices fresh ginger
1 stick cinnamon
sugar to taste

1 Put the figs into a saucepan with the ginger and stick of cinnamon and enough water to just cover. Set aside for 1 hour. Bring slowly to the boil, stir in ½ cup sugar (or more if you like) and dissolve over low heat.
2 Simmer until the figs are soft, and the ginger almost translucent. Serve warm or chilled, with pouring cream.

Rich Bread Pudding with Whisky and Cinnamon Sauce

Lace Cookie Cones. Large plate: Basler Leckerli (page 104) and Cashew and Spice Cake. Small plate: Ginger Cookies (page 104)

Cashew and Spice Cake
(Love Cake)

A rich, sweet and very spicy cake traditionally served at birthdays among the Dutch burgher community of Sri Lanka. There, the cashews are painstakingly chopped by hand. Here is a quicker version. A feature of this cake is its soft, gooey centre so don't worry when you cut into it, this is exactly how it should be. If baked too long or at too high a temperature it loses this soft layer.

PREPARATION TIME: *35 minutes*
COOKING TIME: *1 hour*
MAKES *1 cake, 25 × 30 cm*

6 large eggs
2 cups caster sugar
150 g unsalted butter
250 g raw cashews
250 g semolina
¼ cup honey
*2 tablespoons rose water or ¼ teaspoon
rose essence*
finely chopped zest of 1 lime or lemon
1 teaspoon freshly grated nutmeg
1 teaspoon ground cardamom

1 Line a 25 × 30 cm shallow cake tin with two layers of paper — first greaseproof paper and then non-stick baking paper. Preheat oven to slow (150°C).
2 Beat eggs and sugar on high speed in electric mixer for 10 minutes or until thick and light. Add the soft butter and beat well.
3 Chop cashews in food processor, leaving them at a coarsely chopped stage rather than letting them go to powder. Stir in, together with the semolina, honey, rose water, lime zest, nutmeg and cardamom.
4 Turn mixture into the prepared tin and bake in a slow oven for 1 hour or until pale golden on top. If cake starts to brown too quickly, cover loosely with foil. This cake is meant to be moist and sticky in the centre, so don't rely on the skewer test or it will be overcooked and lose its charm.
5 Leave in the tin to cool. Cut the cake in small squares to remove from the tin — much as you would treat chewy brownies.

Lace Cookie Cones

I've taken the liberty of changing a traditional recipe — brandy snaps — and suggest cone shapes instead of straight rolls. The cream can't escape at the farther end when you bite into one!

PREPARATION TIME: *15 minutes*
COOKING TIME: *30 minutes (4–5 minutes
a batch)*
MAKES *about 24*

60 g butter
3 tablespoons caster sugar
2 tablespoons golden syrup
4½ tablespoons plain flour
1 teaspoon ground ginger
200 mL cream
2 tablespoons finely chopped glacé ginger

1 Preheat oven to moderate (180°C).
2 In a saucepan, gently heat butter, sugar and syrup, stirring until melted. Remove from heat and stir in flour and ginger, sifted together.
3 Put half teaspoons of mixture well apart on a buttered baking tray. Don't cook more than 4 at a time because they have to be shaped while hot. Bake until golden brown, 4–5 minutes.
4 Remove tray from oven and while the next tray is baking, gently lift up each wafer with a spatula and shape into a cone. If you have cream horn forms, use these, but it is very easy to just curl the soft wafers into a cone with your fingers. They become hard and brittle as they cool.
5 When all the mixture is cooked, shaped and rolled, store in an airtight container. They keep well and can be made a few days ahead.
6 Just before they are required, whip cream and stir in chopped glacé ginger. The cream should be just stiff enough to pipe. Fill an icing bag fitted with a large star nozzle and fill the cones. Arrange on a serving plate.

When the Dutch controlled the Spice Islands and their nutmeg trees in the seventeenth century, they made systematic attempts to remove all such trees from other islands to ensure their monopoly. Their efforts were in vain for birds ate the fruits and took the seeds to other places.

Potato Spice Cake

sugar. Peel a piece of fresh ginger root and grate finely. Discard any fibres left on the outside of the grater and measure the grated ginger. Add to the creamed mixture with the golden syrup.

2 Add the egg gradually, stopping if the mixture shows signs of curdling. You may not need all of the beaten egg. Stir in flours and ginger sifted together. The dough will be soft.

3 Wrap the dough in plastic and refrigerate for at least 2 hours. Preheat oven to moderate (180°C) and line baking trays with non-stick baking paper.

4 Take half teaspoons of the dough, roll into small balls and place well apart on the baking trays. Dip the tines of a fork in flour and lightly press each ball to flatten and mark with lines. Bake for 10 minutes or until firm and light brown. Remove to a wire rack and leave until quite cold before storing in an airtight container.

Basler Leckerli

This fruity, nutty slice is very chewy when first baked, but softens after a day or two. Nice both ways, it is a Swiss specialty from Basel.

PREPARATION TIME: *30 minutes plus overnight resting time*
COOKING TIME: *20 minutes*
MAKES *30 squares*

225 g (⅔ cup) honey
150 g sugar
2 teaspoons ground cinnamon
½ teaspoon ground nutmeg
⅛ teaspoon ground cloves
100 g chopped, mixed peel
100 g chopped, blanched almonds
finely grated rind of 1 lemon
50 mL kirsch
300 g plain flour
1 teaspoon baking powder

ICING
150 g icing sugar, sifted
2 tablespoons kirsch or water

1 Put the honey, sugar and spices into a heavy saucepan and bring slowly to the boil.

2 Remove from heat and add the mixed

Ginger Cookies

Here is a crisp cookie with really good flavour. I find those made with the dried spice alone are never quite gingery enough for my taste, so I have included grated fresh ginger for extra oomph.

PREPARATION TIME: *10 minutes plus 2 hours chilling time*
COOKING TIME: *about 20 minutes*
MAKES *about 50 cookies*

90 g unsalted butter
½ cup firmly packed brown sugar
3 teaspoons finely grated fresh ginger
1½ tablespoons golden syrup
1 small egg, beaten
½ cup plain flour
½ cup self-raising flour
2 teaspoons ground ginger

1 Cream softened butter and brown

Anise with its strong licorice flavour and smell is used to saturate a sack, which is then dragged through the countryside as a lure for foxhounds in a drag hunt in England and the United States.

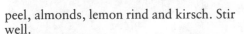

peel, almonds, lemon rind and kirsch. Stir well.

3 Sift the flour and baking powder together and stir into the mixture. Turn out on a marble slab or smooth work surface and knead to mix. The dough should still be warm.

4 Roll out to a rectangular shape 7 mm thick on the back of a baking tray, or pat into a lightly buttered baking tin 30 × 27 cm and 7 mm thick. Leave to rest for a few hours or overnight.

5 Preheat oven to 220°C and bake for 15–20 minutes. Have ready the icing sugar mixed with kirsch or water and spread thinly on the surface as soon as the leckerli is taken from the oven.

6 Trim off any hard edges with a sharp knife and cut into 4 cm squares.

Scandinavian Christmas Bread

A very fragrant bread that's not overly rich. A good addition to the Christmas table — but don't just wait for Christmas, its lovely anytime.

PREPARATION TIME: *1 hour plus rising time* ·
COOKING TIME: *40 minutes*
MAKES *1 loaf*

¾ *cup milk*
½ *cup sugar*
1 *teaspoon salt*
125 *g unsalted butter*
30 *g fresh yeast or 1 sachet active dry yeast*
½ *cup warm water*
4 *cups plain flour*
1 *teaspoon ground cardamom*
¼ *cup chopped mixed peel*
¼ *cup chopped blanched almonds*
¼ *cup sultanas*
¼ *cup quartered glacé cherries*

1 Heat the milk in a saucepan until small bubbles start to form around the side of pan, then remove from heat and stir in the sugar, salt and butter until sugar is dissolved and butter melted. Cool to lukewarm.

2 Sprinkle the yeast over warm water in a large bowl and stir to dissolve yeast. Add the milk mixture. Sift half the flour

with the cardamom and add to liquids, beating well with wooden spoon until smooth.

3 Stir in remaining flour to make a dough. Turn on to a lightly floured surface and knead for 10 minutes or until smooth and elastic. It may be necessary to add a little extra flour.

4 Form dough into a smooth ball and place in a warm greased bowl. Turn dough so the top is greased. Leave in a warm place, covered with a cloth, until dough doubles in bulk, about 1 hour.

5 Punch down dough and on a lightly floured surface knead in the fruits and almonds. Once more form dough into a ball. Place on a large, well greased baking tray. Cover with a cloth and leave in a warm, draught-free place to rise until almost doubled in bulk.

6 Preheat oven to moderately hot (190°C) and bake risen loaf for about 40 minutes. Cover top of bread after 20 minutes to prevent over-browning.

7 Cool on a wire rack. If it is to be kept for any length of time, when completely cold wrap tightly in foil and freeze.

Potato Spice Cake

A cake that uses no butter or eggs but is nicely moist is a recipe to treasure.

PREPARATION TIME: *10 minutes*
COOKING TIME: *1 hour, plus cooking time for potato*
MAKES *1 cake*

1 *cup mashed potato*
1 *cup sugar*
1 *cup sultanas*
1 *cup milk*
1 *teaspoon mixed spice*
2 *cups self-raising flour*

1 Preheat oven to moderate (180°C). In a mixing bowl, combine all the ingredients thoroughly.

2 Grease a 20 cm ring tin or baba mould, spoon mixture into tin, bake 1 hour or until firm and golden. Allow to cool in tin for 10 minutes, then turn out. Serve warm, sliced and buttered if you prefer.

> Ginger is so called because its roots are shaped like the antlers of deer. The name comes from the Sanskrit word meaning 'shaped like a horn'.

Oat and Apple Muffins

Speculaas

These spiced cookies are also known as St Nicholas biscuits and are traditional in Holland for the feast of St Nicholas early in December.

PREPARATION TIME: *45 minutes*
COOKING TIME: *10 minutes*
MAKES *about 36 cookies*

1 cup plain flour
2 teaspoons baking powder
2 teaspooons ground cinnamon
½ teaspoon ground cloves
½ teaspoon ground nutmeg
¼ teaspoon ground aniseed
¼ teaspoon ground ginger
¼ teaspoon ground black pepper
¼ teaspoon salt
125 g butter
¾ cup firmly packed brown sugar
1 tablespoon rum or milk

1 Preheat oven to moderately hot (190°C).
2 Sift together flour, baking powder, spices and salt. Cream the butter and sugar until light and creamy. Stir in milk or rum, then gradually add the sifted ingredients and knead to a soft dough.
2 Roll out on a lightly floured board to 3 mm thickness and cut into rectangular shapes. Using a spatula, carefully transfer to buttered baking trays and bake in a moderately hot oven for 10 minutes or until golden brown. Cool and store in an airtight container.

Cardamom Butter Balls

A sweet, sugar-dusted treat flavoured with cardamom.

PREPARATION TIME: *30 minutes*
COOKING TIME: *12 minutes*
MAKES *about 36*

125 g soft butter
½ cup caster sugar
1 egg
1 cup plain flour
¼ cup cornflour

1 teaspoon ground cardamom
1 teaspoon baking powder
sifted icing sugar

1 Preheat oven to moderately slow (160°C).
2 Cream butter and sugar together until light, then beat in egg. Sift together flour, cornflour, cardamom and baking powder and mix into the creamed mixture. Chill for a few minutes in the refrigerator to stiffen the mixture for shaping.
3 Roll teaspoons of the dough into balls, place on lightly greased baking trays and bake for 12 minutes, or until firm but not brown.
4 While still warm, roll in sifted icing sugar. Cool on a rack and store in an airtight container.

Oat and Apple Muffins

These light and moist muffins, fragrant with cardamom, are a true low cholesterol recipe as they contain no dairy products and use only the whites of eggs. Use any flavourless light oil such as sunflower, maize or grapeseed.

PREPARATION TIME: 10 minutes
COOKING TIME: 20 minutes
MAKES 12 muffins

1 cup self-raising flour
¼ teaspoon salt
2 teaspoons baking powder
1 teaspoon ground cardamom or cinnamon
1 cup oat bran
⅓ cup sugar
1 small apple, peeled and chopped
2 egg whites
¾ cup apple juice
¼ cup light oil

1 Preheat oven to hot (200°C). Brush muffin tins with a little oil.
2 Sift flour, salt, baking powder and cardamom together into a mixing bowl. Stir in the oat bran, sugar and chopped apple until evenly distributed.
3 In a separate bowl beat the egg whites with a fork, add the apple juice and oil and stir. Pour into the dry ingredients and mix lightly with a fork until combined.
4 Put tablespoons of the mixture into muffin cups to three-quarters fill them

and bake in a hot oven (200°C) for 18–20 minutes or until the muffins are well risen and golden brown. Turn out on a wire rack. Serve warm. These muffins also freeze well.

Spiced Prune and Apple Cake

A moist cake with good keeping qualities.

PREPARATION TIME: 15 minutes
COOKING TIME: 50–60 minutes
MAKES 1 loaf cake

1 cup chopped, pitted prunes
1 cup diced apple (1 large)
1 cup chopped walnuts
¾ cup brown sugar
½ cup melted butter
1 tablespoon honey
1 teaspoon bicarbonate of soda
1 tablespoon boiling water
2 eggs well beaten
1½ cups plain flour
1 teaspoon cinnamon
1 teaspoon allspice or nutmeg

1 Preheat oven to 180°C, grease and line a loaf tin.
2 Combine the prunes, apples, walnuts and brown sugar in a medium bowl.
3 Melt the butter and stir in honey while it is still hot, to melt the honey. Dissolve bicarbonate of soda in boiling water and mix with the honey. Add beaten eggs, pour over the fruit and sugar and mix.
4 Sift the dry ingredients and stir into the mixture until well combined. Pour into the prepared tin.
5 Bake in a moderate oven (180°C) for 50–60 minutes until cake is nicely browned and a skewer inserted in centre comes out clean. Cool a few minutes in tin before turning out on cake cooler. If desired, before baking sprinkle cake with an additional teaspoon of sugar combined with ½ teaspoon of cinnamon.

It is not always the strongly flavoured spice which is better. For instance, cinnamon is sweet and mildly fragrant, but sad to say, much of what passes for cinnamon is in reality cassia, which is much stronger. Cassia is also known as Chinese cinnamon, bastard cinnamon or false cinnamon. In the United States, however, it is used widely and what is labelled cinnamon is almost always cassia.

Nutmeg can be sweetly fragrant when freshly grated, or when the ground nutmeg you buy is of good quality and has been correctly packaged, preferably in glass, or it can be a brown dust with but a faint hint of the true character of nutmeg.

Glossary

Although the enjoyment of food is common to all nations, the names by which we know even the most common ingredients can vary from country to country. What Australians call a capsicum is a pepper in England and a bell pepper in America. To compound the problem, food terms travel – with immigrants, foreign visitors and on food packaging – so even within one country, an item may be known by several different names. Consult the chart to locate an unfamiliar ingredient. Where there is no exact equivalent, an alternative my be suggested.

Fish and meat pose special problems. Because America and Britain share a common ocean, some species of fish are common to both (albeit under different names) but many Australian species are unique. Where possible, recipes describe fish in general rather than specific terms; where a specific type of fish is recommended, a reputable fishmonger will be able to suggest a suitable alternative based upon the cooking method.

There is no standard international method for butchering meat, so cuts vary. The glossary lists some equivalents/substitutes. For more advice, consult your butcher.

Australia	UK	US
Dairy Produce		
cream[1]	single cream	light cream
thickened cream	double cream	heavy cream
sour cream	soured cream	dairy sour cream
lard (animal origin)	lard (animal origin)	use shortening (vegetable origin)
bocconcini	small fresh mozzarella cheeses	small fresh mozzarella cheeses
Romano/Pecorino cheese	Pecorino cheese	Romano cheese
Swiss cheese	Emmenthal cheese	Swiss cheese
tasty cheese	mature Cheddar cheese	sharp Cheddar cheese
eggs, hard-boiled	eggs, hard-boiled	eggs, hard-cooked

[1]The range of creams sold commercially is constantly increasing. Crème fraîche is a cultured thick cream with a slightly sour tang.

Ingredients for Baking		
plain flour	plain flour	all-purpose flour[1]
self-raising flour	self-raising flour	self-rising flour
wholemeal flour	wholemeal flour	Graham/wholewheat flour
cornflour	cornflour	cornstarch
polenta/maize flour	yellow cornmeal	yellow cornmeal
bicarbonate of soda	bicarbonate of soda	baking soda
compressed yeast	fresh yeast	compressed yeast
white crystal sugar	white granulated sugar	white sugar[2]
caster sugar	caster sugar	superfine/extrafine sugar[2]
icing sugar	icing sugar	confectioners'/powdered sugar
demerara sugar	demerara sugar	use light brown sugar
raw sugar	use Muscovado sugar	use Turbinado sugar
golden syrup	golden syrup	use light corn syrup or maple syrup
molasses	use black treacle	molasses

[1]American flour is finely milled – for baking, it may be necessary to add slightly more fat and liquid for similar results. [2]American regular sugar is finer than the UK equivalent; in most instances it can safely be substituted for caster sugar.

Australia	UK	US
Fresh and Dried Fruit, Vegetables, Herbs and Aromatics		
currants	blackcurrants	black currants
custard apple	custard apple	cherimoya[1]
feijoa	feijoa	feijoa/pineapple guava
galangal	[2]	[2]
kiwifruit	kiwifruit	kiwi/Chinese gooseberry
papaya	pawpaw	papaya
passionfruit	passionfruit	passionfruit/purple granadilla
persimmon	use Sharon fruit	persimmon
rambutans[3]	use lychees	use litchis
rock melon	cantaloupe	cantaloupe
tamarillo[4]	tamarillo/tree tomato	tamarillo/tree tomato
glacé cherry	glacé cherry	candied cherry
sultana	sultana	golden/white raisin
aubergine	aubergine	eggplant
beetroot	beetroot	beet
black-eyed bean	black-eyed bean	black-eyed pea
broad bean	broad bean	fava bean/European broad bean
butternut pumpkin	butternut pumpkin	butternut squash
capsicum	pepper	sweet/bell pepper
capsicum (canned pieces/slices)	pimiento	pimiento
celeriac	celeriac	celery root/celeriac/celeri-rave
chick peas	chick peas	garbanzos/chick peas
choko	chayote/christophene	chayote squash
coriander (fresh)	coriander (fresh)	cilantro
cos lettuce	cos lettuce	romaine lettuce
creamed corn (canned)	cream-style corn (canned)	cream-style corn (canned)
endive/curly endive	endive	chicory
English spinach	spinach	spinach
fennel	fennel	fennel/finocchio
green squash	use pattypan squash	use pattypan squash
haricot beans (dried)	haricot beans (dried)	dried navy beans/Great Northern beans
lamb's lettuce	lamb's lettuce	corn salad
lima beans (dried)	butter beans	lima beans
orange sweet potato/kumara	orange-fleshed sweet potato	sweet potato/yam[5]
potato chips	potato chips	French fries
silver beet	Swiss chard	Swiss chard
snow peas	mangetout	snow peas
snow pea sprouts	use bean sprouts	snow pea sprouts
spring onions	spring onions	scallions
sugar peas	sugarsnaps	sugarsnaps
swede	swede	rutabaga
witloof/chicory	chicory	Belgian endive
zucchini	courgette	zucchini

[1]The term custard apple is used to describe a family of fruit including cherimoya, soursop and sweet sop. [2]Galangal is a rhizome resembling ginger but with a distinctly different flavour. It is not widely known in the UK or the US; ginger can be substituted, but the flavour will not be authentic. [3]Rambutans resemble lychees/litchis in flavour and are sometimes called hairy lychees, because the skin of the small oval fruit is covered with dark red-brown hairy spikes. [4]Tamarillos are smooth-skinned oval fruit, red or yellow in colour. The tough skin must be peeled before use. [5]Although it is customary for Americans to refer to orange-fleshed sweet potatoes as yams, this can cause confusion as true yams are white-fleshed tuberous roots.

Australia	UK	US
Baked Goods and Pastry		
cookie/biscuit	biscuit	cookie
cream cracker	cream cracker	oyster cracker
golden oatmeal biscuits (for crumb crusts)	use digestive biscuits	use Graham crackers
scone	scone	biscuit
sponge finger biscuit	boudoir biscuit	ladyfinger
shortcrust pastry	shortcrust pastry	basic pie dough
filo pastry	filo pastry	phyllo leaves
Nuts, Seeds and Grains		
copha	solid coconut cream	coconut butter
desiccated coconut	desiccated coconut	use shredded coconut
hazelnuts	hazelnuts	filberts/hazelnuts
pine nuts	pine nuts/pine kernels	pignoli/pinenuts
pepitas	dried untoasted pumpkin seeds	dried untoasted pumpkin seeds
burghul	bulgur/parboiled hulled cracked wheat	bulgur
cracked/kibbled wheat	cracked wheat	cracked wheat
Meat and Fish (see also general introduction)		
bacon rashers	bacon rashers	bacon slices/strips
back bacon	back bacon	Canadian bacon
streaky bacon	streaky bacon	bacon[1]
belly of pork	belly of pork	fresh pork sides
blade or round steak	use stewing steak	blade or round steak
boneless chicken breasts	chicken breast fillets	chicken cutlets/suprêmes
cabanossi	smoked sausage with garlic and spices	smoked sausage with garlic and spices
coppa	cured ham[2]	cured ham[2]
corned silverside	salted silverside	corned beef
ham steaks	gammon steaks	ham steaks
kassler	lightly salted pork loin smoked with juniper berries	lightly salted pork smoked with juniper berries or top round
minced meat	minced meat	ground meat[3]
offal	offal	variety meats
pancetta	cured pork sausage	cured pork sausage
pork fillet	pork fillet	pork tenderloin
sausage mince	sausagemeat	sausagemeat
topside roast	beef topside	use round rump roast
king prawns	king prawns	jumbo shrimp
prawns[4]	prawns	shrimp
shrimp	shrimp	baby/cocktail shrimp

[1]Packaged American sliced bacon is cut very thinly; substitute 3 slices for every 2 rashers listed in recipes. [2]Coppa is an Italian cured ham, fattier than Prosciutto, from the shoulder and the neck of the pig. [3]Americans sometimes refer to ground beef as hamburger. [4]The term 'green prawns' is sometimes used to describe raw prawns.

Storecupboard Items

cooking chocolate	cooking chocolate/Menière	unsweetened baking chocolate
dark chocolate	plain chocolate	semisweet chocolate
milk chocolate	milk chocolate	sweet chocolate
choc bits	use chocolate chips	use chocolate chips
chocolate vermicelli/hail	chocolate vermicelli	chocolate sprinkles
hundreds and thousands	hundreds and thousands	nonpareil
jelly crystals	jelly cubes	flavoured gelatin[1]
shoyu/tamari	naturally fermented soy sauce	naturally fermented soy sauce
stock cubes	stock cubes	bouillon cubes[2]
tomato purée	passata	tomato purée
tomato paste	tomato purée (concentrate)	tomato paste
tomato sauce	thin puréed tomatoes	tomato sauce
vanilla bean	vanilla pod	vanilla bean
vanilla essence	vanilla essence	vanilla extract[3]

[1]Jelly (the dessert, not the preserve) comes as crystals or cubes. Check package instructions when making up in case the amount of liquid required is different from that specified in recipes. [2]Some bouillon cubes are only half the size of regular stock cubes; check the labelling for the amount of liquid to use. [3]Vanilla essence/extract comes in different strengths; add to taste. Use natural vanilla essence where possible.

Appliances, Cookware and Paper Products

absorbent paper	kitchen paper	paper towels
bar pan	loaf tin	loaf pan
double saucepan	double saucepan	double boiler
frying pan	frying pan	skillet
greaseproof paper	greaseproof paper	use waxed paper or baking parchment
griller	grill	broiler[1]
Lamington tin	28 x 18 cm /11 x 7 in baking tray, 4 cm/1½ in deep	28 x 18 cm/11 x 7 in baking tray, 4 cm/1½ in deep
patty cases	paper cake cases	cupcake papers
plastic wrap	cling film	plastic wrap
sandwich cake tin	sandwich cake tin	layer cake pan
springform tin	spring-release tin	springform pan
Swiss roll tin	Swiss roll tin	jelly roll pan
tea-towel	tea-towel	dish-towel
toothpick	cocktail stick	toothpick

[1]Where Australian and British cooks talk about grilling, Americans use the term broiling, except for barbecued food, which is grilled in all three countries.